A Brief History of the Book

A Brief History of the Book

From Tablet to Tablet

Steven K. Galbraith

LIBRARIES
UNLIMITED®
An Imprint of ABC-CLIO, LLC
Santa Barbara, California • Denver, Colorado

Library of Congress Cataloging-in-Publication Data

Names: Galbraith, Steven K., author.
Title: A brief history of the book : from tablet to tablet / Steven K. Galbraith.
Description: Santa Barbara, California : Libraries Unlimited, [2020] | Includes
    bibliographical references and index.
Identifiers: LCCN 2020014986 (print) | LCCN 2020014987 (ebook) | ISBN 9781440869396
    (paperback ; acid-free paper) | ISBN 9781440869402 (ebook)
Subjects: LCSH: Books—History. | Writing materials and instruments—History. |
    Written communication—History. | Pocket computers. | Electronic book readers. |
    Books—History—Problems, exercises, etc.
Classification: LCC Z4 .G25 2020 (print) | LCC Z4 (ebook) | DDC 002.09—dc23
LC record available at https://lccn.loc.gov/2020014986
LC ebook record available at https://lccn.loc.gov/2020014987

ISBN: 978-1-4408-6939-6 (paperback)
      978-1-4408-6940-2 (ebook)

24 23 22 21 20   1 2 3 4 5

This book is also available as an eBook.

Libraries Unlimited
An Imprint of ABC-CLIO, LLC

ABC-CLIO, LLC
147 Castilian Drive
Santa Barbara, California 93117
www.abc-clio.com

This book is printed on acid-free paper ∞

Manufactured in the United States of America

Dedicated to the memory of John W. Ellison

Contents

Acknowledgments

A Brief History of the Book would not have been possible without the Cary Graphic Arts Collection at RIT and my wonderful work colleagues there: Amelia Fontanel, David Pankow, Shani Avni, Lauren Alberque, Gregory Decker, and Ella Von Holtum. Research for the book was facilitated by the resourceful and patient Morna Hilderbrand and the IDS Department of RIT's Wallace Library. For their photography and design talents, I am indebted to Elizabeth Lamark, Blayke Morrow, Jiageng Lin, Marnie Soom, Jenna Nichols, Jordan Funk, and Amelia Fontanel (again!).

From Libraries Unlimited, I need to thank Barbara Ittner for encouraging me to get this book started and Emma Bailey for encouraging me to get it finished.

I want to thank my friend Chuck Bigelow for his words of encouragement.

Finally, I wish to thank my family: Jeannie, Audrey, Maddie, Jim, Diane, Annie, Cooper, Sam, John, Ginger, Jill, Andy, Lisa, Kamden, Noella, and Mary for all of their love and support.

Introduction

From ancient clay and wax tablets, to papyrus rolls, to medieval manuscript books, to printed books, and to tablet computers, books have taken a great variety of forms over the past five millennia.

As I write this introduction I have an iPhone in my pocket. Many of you reading this book probably have an iPhone or another smartphone nearby. According to the Pew Research Center, as of 2018, 77 percent of Americans own a smartphone.[1] Perhaps you have a tablet computer with you—53 percent of Americans own a tablet computer.[2] How are you reading this book? Is it a printed paperback, or is it a Kindle? All of these reading technologies, all of these forms of the book, inherit aspects of a long history of reading and writing technology that begins back in about 3200 BCE.[3]

When scholars present the history of the book, they might choose to focus on books in the form in which we know them best—the codex. A codex, in its most basic form, are leaves of paper, or another substrate, gathered together and bound along the long edge so that it can be opened and closed and the pages can be turned. A textbook on the history of the book might start with European medieval manuscript books and work forward through the invention of Gutenberg's system of printing and beyond. Increasingly, however, history of the book courses are looking further back and taking a more global approach. *A Brief History of the Book: From Tablet to Tablet* begins with the tablets of the ancient world and then moves forward to the tablets of today. Tablet to tablet—cuneiform to Kindle. In between are 5,000 years of the evolution of the book.

Throughout *A Brief History of the Book*, the term "book" will be used in its most inclusive way, expanding its definition to a variety of technologies that present texts and images to readers. This definition owes much to influential scholars in the field of the history of the book. D. F. McKenzie, for example, helped set the groundwork for the modern study of books, launching a "discipline that studies texts as recorded forms, and the processes of their transmission, including their production and reception."[4] He expanded the definition of texts "to include all forms of texts, not merely books or . . . signs on pieces of parchment or paper." In a similar fashion, *A Brief History of the Book* will approach books in a broader way that allows us to begin with the very first written communication and travel all the way to the very present.

Five thousand years in one brief book? How is this possible? It is not. *A Brief History of the Book: From Tablet to Tablet* is, as the title suggests, a brief history and not meant to be comprehensive. This book presents a chronology of some of the major forms that the book has taken, introducing the reader to many of the most important developments in the history of the book. Throughout that history, certain themes emerge that demonstrate how writing and reading technologies are a part of a long evolution, with one technology informing the next—old influencing the new (and occasionally the new influencing the old). Although the materials, texts, and readers change, the nature and use of these technologies have consistencies that have endured for over five millennia.

As a curator, I teach with artifacts. This approach extends to writing, as well. Throughout *A Brief History of the Book*, historical examples are provided from the Cary Graphic Arts Collection at Rochester Institute of Technology (RIT), where I serve as curator. Established in 1969 as a part of RIT's School of Printing, our special collections library documents the history of graphic communication. Due to its foundational connections with RIT's printing curriculum, the Cary Collection (for short) has a particularly strong focus on the history of the printed book. Over the decades of its relatively short existence, the library has sought to expand its scope, so our collection increasingly documents a more comprehensive history. Like most libraries in the United States and Europe that focus on the history of the book, the core of our collection reflects the Western tradition. In an effort to expand the scope to better exhibit a greater global history, the Cary Collection continues to diversify its holdings.

A Brief History of the Book is written for courses in fields such as library science, English literature, and history. It is a *brief* history that follows primarily the evolution from the cuneiform tablets of ancient Babylon and Sumer to today's digital tablets. Forms of the book presented along this evolution have been chosen both for their impact on this history and the accessibility of such objects for students for primary study. The artifacts presented are hopefully ones that can be seen and handled in collaboration with a local library, archive, or museum. Supporting a hands-on approach, *A Brief History of the Book* features exercises that can be achieved in most classrooms and are appropriate for students of all ages.

MODERN ADS FOR EARLY TECHNOLOGIES

As we examine each new technology in the history of the book, we will note important themes that carry through the history of the book from the ancient world all the way to the present, including: memory, readable/writable, recyclability, durability, security, cost, and style of access. To exemplify these themes in a modern, accessible manner, *A Brief History of the Book: From Tablet to Tablet* presents playful, modern advertisements for historical technologies. These ads are admittedly anachronistic and certainly a little silly, but they help in analyzing important themes, as well as similarities in technologies from ancient to modern.

Memory: How much information does the technology hold? When we look at modern technologies, storage or memory is a very important consideration. How much information does the device hold? The answer is usually represented in bytes (KB, MB, GB, TB). Such a measurement does not literally translate to earlier analog technology, but by evoking a comparable estimate in page numbers, volumes, or even bytes we might achieve a figurative sense of memory capacity.

Readable/Writable: This category asks: when using this technology, can text be written, modified, and/or erased?

Recyclability: Can the technology be recycled and reused in some form?

Durability: How long will the book last?

Security: Does the book form have a way of protecting the information it contains?

Access: This refers to the manner in which the reader accesses information presented when using books. For example, we will compare random access to linear access.

Cost: How much does it cost to produce or purchase the book? Here we will follow the kind of infographics often used for restaurant guides. The more dollar signs, the more expensive the book technology.

This approach might strike you as a little anachronistic. But approaching historical book forms, even ancient ones, in this manner reveals the commonalities between ancient and modern, and all that we find in between. Such comparisons might also reveal what books might look like in future, and how reading and writing might change in the years to come. When students come to the Cary Collection at Rochester Institute of Technology and learn about book history, I often get the sense that some of them may just be the ones who shape the future of the book. Or perhaps it will be some of the readers of this book.

OVERVIEW OF CHAPTERS

A Brief History of the Book: From Tablet to Tablet is presented in four chapters, each covering important developments in the evolution of the book.

Chapter One, "The Ancient World," begins in about 3200 BCE with clay cuneiform tablets found in Mesopotamian civilizations such as Sumer and Old Babylon. We then travel to Egypt at about the same period of time and explore rolls (or scrolls) made from papyrus harvested from the banks of the Nile River. Moving ahead to about 1250 BCE, we examine the use of wax tablets, a technology found in ancient Greece and Rome that endures through the European Middle Ages. Chapter One concludes with hands-on activities for making and using clay and wax tablets.

Chapter Two, "Early Printing and Medieval Manuscripts," picks up the narrative with the invention of paper in China in the beginning of the second century CE. This invention inspires woodblock printing in about the seventh century CE that spreads from China through Japan and Korea. Returning to the Middle East and Europe, we discuss the use of parchment as a writing material and the rise of the codex in the fourth century CE. Moving into the European Middle Ages, we examine how manuscript books were produced, from the preparation of the parchment through to the binding of the book.

Chapter Three, "Printing with Movable Type," begins with the invention of movable type in China by Bì Shēng in approximately 1040 CE. We then travel to Mainz, Germany, in the mid-15th century to examine Johannes Gutenberg's invention of printing using a wooden press and movable type cast in a hand mold. We investigate the production of a printed book including typefounding, typesetting, and the operation of a hand press. The development of the printed book and its common features is then described, with attention paid to the earliest years of printing—the incunabula period, or printing prior to 1501. Printing with a hand press remained a relatively unchanged technology until the 19th century, when book production became industrialized. Mechanized innovations in type-founding and printing are explored, as well as the fine press printing movement that emerged as a reaction to industrialization. Chapter Three concludes with activities that provide experience with setting movable type from a type case into a composing stick, and writing the history of a book.

Chapter Four, "Digital Books," opens with a history of modern digital tablets that presents a progressive sequence of personal computers, portable computers, personal digital assistants, e-readers, smartphones, and tablet computers. The history of the World Wide Web is considered in relationship to the evolution of the book, including a brief exploration of incunabula websites. We then contemplate the future of books by looking at innovations using virtual and augmented reality, as well as new printed forms. Chapter Four concludes with a hands-on activity using the Graffiti handwriting system on a Palm Pilot and comparing that experience to impressing characters in a clay tablet.

NOTES

1. https://www.pewinternet.org/fact-sheet/mobile.

2. Ibid.

3. This book uses the system BCE (Before the Common Era) and CE (Common Era) rather than BC and AD.

4. D. F. Mckenzie, *Bibliography and the Sociology of Texts* (London: British Library, 1986), 4.

ONE

The Ancient World

CUNEIFORM TABLETS

Natural resources determine much of the history of the book. The world's earliest books emerged from the riverbanks of ancient Mesopotamia. Scribes in areas such as Sumer and Babylon (roughly now the location of southern Iraq) gathered clay and fashioned it into small, handheld tablets into which symbols could be incised or impressed with a stylus. This system of writing is called cuneiform. Dating back to the latter part of the fourth millennium BCE (3200 BCE is often a cited date), cuneiform was used for ancient languages such Sumerian and Akkadian.[1] The word "cuneiform" is rooted in the Latin "cuneus" meaning "wedge." Combine "cuneus" with "form," and the term simply means wedge-form or wedge-shaped. This refers to the impression made when a stylus is pressed into the wet clay.

The process of making a clay tablet is captured in this translation of a surviving account of a school exercise in Old Babylon.

[Qu]ick, come here, take the clay,

knead it, flatten it,

[Calc]ulate (the amount needed), fold it (over itself),

reinforce the core, form (the tablet),

[. . .] plan it, [. . .]

hurry, [. . .]

lift up the flap-clay, trim it off![2]

Clay, an accessible and abundant natural resource, was shaped by hand into a tablet for use as a writing surface. The size and shape of cuneiform tablets varied, and often depended on the text that was to be written, but they were typically square or rectangular, and small enough to hold in one's hand. Cuneiform tablets were held in the hand when written on, and they rested in the hand when read. Scholars often note a writing surface "about the size of a credit card but around 1 cm thick."[3]

Throughout the course of the history of books, the quality of the writing material might depend on what sort of book was being produced. In the medieval period, for example, a finer grade of parchment (animal skin) might be chosen for a more luxurious manuscript book. Similarly, a finer paper might be chosen for a more luxurious printed book. As Finkel and Taylor note, the same was true for the clay used for tablets: "Scribes always knew where to find the right quality of clay for their needs. Ephemeral documents could be written on rougher clay, while library tablets could be written on finer clay, sometimes so smoothly finished as to look like porcelain."[4]

The tool used for writing on the earliest tablets was a pointed stylus used to draw pictographs into the clay. Later on, as writing systems evolved, the tool used for impressing cuneiform characters into clay was made by cutting a slender, three-sided stylus out of the side of a reed. Its shape is akin to that of an isosceles triangle, though with one of the long sides curved (the rounded part of the reed). A reed might also have been cut to create a shape that was more like an arc with squared corners at the edges used to impress a wedge-shape in the clay.[5]

As shown in figure 1-1, the scribe held the clay tablet in one hand and the stylus in the other. Before writing, the scribe might have prepared the tablet by ruling the surface of the clay using the long edge of a stylus or a piece of string.[6] Ruling a writing surface, of course, helps organize and guide handwriting. It is a common practice across the history

Figure 1-1　A scribe creates a cuneiform tablet. A display from The New York Times Museum of the Recorded Word. RIT Cary Graphic Arts Collection. Photograph by Jiageng Lin.

of writing and still continues today with ruled paper. Symbols were impressed while the clay was still wet. The tablet was then left to air dry. As water contained in the clay evaporated, the tablet hardened enough so that the writing inscribed in it became stabilized. When handling a surviving cuneiform tablet, one might get the sense that it had been baked at some point. That was rarely the case in ancient times. Surviving cuneiform tablets either have hardened solid over time or were baked at a later date to better preserve them.

Evolution of Cuneiform

As mentioned earlier, the earliest cuneiform tablets were not impressed with triangular reeds, but rather incised with styluses with pointed tips.[7] The glyphs used were not symbolic characters, but pictographs representing things. Looking ahead to an exercise for this chapter, you can view the evolution of the symbol for barley (figure 1-2). In about 3100 BCE, the symbol was a pictograph of barley drawn with a pointed tip. Moving forward to 700 BCE, the symbol had become abstracted; barley is represented by a combination of four wedge-shaped impressions. On the one hand, part of this evolution is owed to humans adapting the technology. On the other hand, part is owed to humans adapting *to* the technology. As Taylor notes, "Curved lines are gradually replaced by impressed wedges, and the script assumes a more abstract appearance. Speed and ease of writing and the greater visibility of wedges with larger heads (thus, impressed) may be among the reasons for this transition."[8] Take, for example, the early symbol for barley. Incising this pictorial symbol into clay with a sharpened edge would take a total of nine strokes. Also, because the thin lines would have been incised with a pointed instrument, the impressions left behind would not be as legible or clean—drawing in clay in this manner leaves debris along the edges of the lines. Impressing the symbol for barley in cuneiform is noticeably easier. Rather than nine strokes, it requires only four clean, legible impressions.

Books always need a source of illumination in order to be read, whether the sun, a candle, or electric lamp. These are all sources of external light. Modern tablets often use internal light sources for their screens. With cuneiform, sunlight illuminates the wedged-shaped writing. As Finkel and Taylor note, "Scribes read by holding the tablet in such a way that sunlight cast shadows into the wedges."[9] The shadows reveal the characters, making them legible.

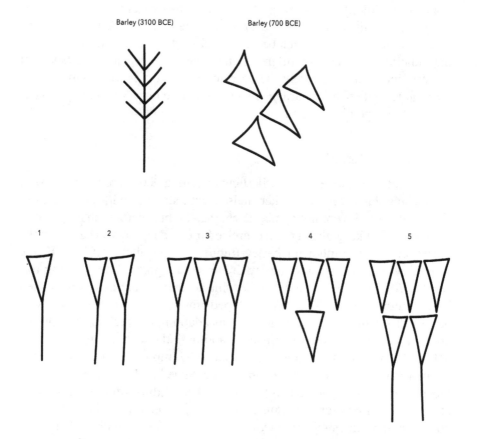

Barley (3100 BCE)   Barley (700 BCE)

1   2   3   4   5

Figure 1-2   The evolution of barley and counting 1 to 5 in cuneiform. Illustration by Blayke Morrow.

AN EXAMPLE FROM THE CARY COLLECTION

A Sumerian tablet (c. 2100 BCE) held at the Cary Collection is shown in figure 1-3. This example is somewhat larger than typical cuneiform tablets. In fact, it measures 4.75×3 inches (12.2 cm×7.8 cm), about the size of an average modern smartphone. The text written on the tablet is an accounting of a crop yield.[10] Information found on many early cuneiform tablets indicates that they were first used for accounting and taking stock of inventories. As Casson writes, "The contents of the earliest clay tablets are simple notations of numbers of commodities—animals, jars, baskets, etc. Writing, it would appear, started as a primitive form of bookkeeping."[11] Because of this, early language tended mostly to be concrete nouns and numbers.[12] As writing evolved, cuneiform would be used for legal contracts, letters, religious documents, and, later on, historical narratives. Reading as a pastime had not yet developed. As Robson succinctly puts it, "There is no early Mesopotamian evidence of reading for pleasure . . ."[13]

Figure 1-3 A Sumerian cuneiform tablet from c. 2100. RIT Cary Graphic Arts Collection. Photograph by Elizabeth Lamark.

Colophons and Curses

For modern readers, title pages are the location for finding information about books. Typically, this includes the name of the author, title of the work, publisher, place of publication, and year of publication. Title pages do not become commonplace in books until the 16th century. Prior to the development of title pages, information about books was often found at ends of texts in a colophon. Deriving from the Greek word meaning "finishing touch" or "finishing stroke," colophons are written statements that provide information about the text.[14] Colophons are commonly used in medieval manuscripts, early printed books, and modern artists' books. The origin of the colophon dates to cuneiform tablets, which sometimes included a statement at the end of text that identifies the scribe, the date of tablet, and where it was created.[15] For longer texts that required multiple tablets, the colophon might record its "place in the sequence" and write out "the first line of the next tablet."[16] This ensured that a series of tablets were read in the correct order. Similar organizational features would later be used in manuscript and printed books. (See signatures and catchwords in Chapters Two and Three.)

Occasionally, colophons included information of a much graver nature. In an attempt to ward off those who might potentially steal or intentionally damage a tablet, the scribe might inscribe a curse. For example, a surviving Assyrian tablet from c. 650 BCE ends with this weighty warning:

> He who breaks this tablet or puts it in water or rubs it until you cannot recognize it [and] cannot make it be understood, may Ashur, Sin, Shamash, Adad and Ishtar, Bel, Nergal, Ishtar of Nineveh, Ishtar of Arbela, Ishtar of Bit Kidmurri, the gods of heaven and earth and the gods of Assyria, may all these curse him with a curse which cannot be relieved, terrible and merciless, as long as he lives, may they let his name, his seed, be carried off from the land, may they put his flesh in a dog's mouth.[17]

This dramatic and rather detailed curse seems an effective notice for any who would dare mar the tablet. Another example of a curse, this time from the temple of Eshtar in Uruk, blesses those who respectfully use the tablet, while cursing those who might steal it:

> The scholar who does not change a line and puts (this tablet back) in the library . . . , may Eshtar look favorably on him! But he who takes (it) out of the Eanna, may Eshtar assail him in anger.[18]

Curses added to texts as a means of protection from potential thieves are found in books for centuries to come. Housed in the Cary Collection, for example, is an English book from 1632 titled *Cyrupaedia: The Institution and Life of Cyrus*. Written on its front paste-down leaf is one of the more common book curses used during the medieval and early modern periods in Europe:

> Steal not this Book my honest friend
> For fear the gallows be your end
> For when you die the Lord will say
> Where is the book you stole away?[19]

Owners of printed copies of *A Brief History of the Book: From Tablet to Tablet* might consider protecting their book by inscribing a curse somewhere in its preliminary pages. Those reading a copy on their Kindle might consider applying a sticker to the back of their device that reads: "Steal not this Kindle honest friend . . ."

Reuse and Recycling

The curses above found on cuneiform tablets mention putting tablets in water or changing a line. This speaks to the reusable nature of clay. During the ancient period, clay tablets were typically air dried and therefore not fully hardened. Rewetting a tablet could make the clay once again malleable. Thus, when information on tablets was no longer needed, the clay could be rewetted and used again for a new purpose. As Charpin notes, "That practice is primarily attested in schools, but also in administration archives. The scribes, having drawn up a summation, could reuse the clay of the small tablets written day to day. . . . There are also cases in which an individual who was traveling, needing to reply to a letter, reused the clay from the tablet he had received."[20]

Looking again at the Sumerian tablet, c. 2100 BCE (figure 1-3), you might notice the blank areas on the tablet. These are likely areas left for further writing that was never accomplished. In this way, cuneiform tablets were not a fixed writing surface, but a reusable resource.

Security

Due to their malleable nature, some cuneiform tablets needed to be enclosed to protect their texts from manipulation or keep their contents private. The technology used to seal a cuneiform tablet was a clay envelope. In the same way that our modern paper envelopes protect letters and keep their contents safe and private, cuneiform tablets could be wrapped in a thin envelope of clay for the same purposes. For example, figure 1-4 shows a Sumerian tablet (c. 2300 BCE) that rests inside a protective clay envelope. This tablet measures 1.75×1.68 inches (4.5×4.3 cm). At some point in its life, a side of this tablet's envelope was broken off, revealing a section of the tablet within. If you look carefully, you can see that there is a tiny gap between the envelope and the tablet. Knowing that both the clay tablet and envelope are still somewhat pliable, it might be tricky to construct an envelope without marring the text on the tablet. A likely solution

Figure 1-4 A Sumerian cuneiform tablet in a clay envelope from c. 2300. RIT Cary Graphic Arts Collection. Photograph by Elizabeth Lamark.

to this challenge was air-drying the tablet prior to wrapping it in the envelope; that way the two were less likely to attach to each other.[21]

This particular tablet is a labor contract, as revealed from the summation of the tablet recorded on the envelope; there is not enough text showing on the visible tablet inside to comprehend its text. On the outside of the envelope is also a seal that identifies the main party involved. This was created by a stone cylinder that was carefully carved with the text and image that served administratively as an official signature.[22] When this cylinder was rolled onto a tablet, it left a relief impression of its engraving in the clay.

Considering that this tablet is a contract, protecting the text meant protecting the contract. If there were some sort of dispute, the envelope could be opened and the tablet read, the concerned parties safe in the knowledge that the text had not been altered. In the history of communication technology, the clay envelope might be the first information security system—an ancient firewall.

Circulation

Cuneiform tablets were not circulated in the same way other books would be in the centuries to come. They were not produced for an audience and sold, nor did they circulate very widely. Very few people made them, and very few people read them. There were professional scribes, trained in the art, who created tablets usually for administrative purposes.[23] The history of the book has a parallel history of literacy. As communication technology evolved, so too did its uses and the number of those people who engaged with it.

Storage

Due to the ephemeral nature of their texts, cuneiform tablets typically had short lives. Once their usefulness had expired, tablets could be erased for reuse, soaked and reformed into new tablets or other clay objects, or simply discarded. Surviving tablets that are found in situ, that is, where they were kept by their original owners, suggest that they were often stored in baskets, ceramic pots, or on shelves (or found lying in a manner that indicates that they had once rested on shelves that had deteriorated). Sometimes tablets survived in groups.[24] In fact, evidence shows that tablets were collected in temple libraries.[25] A recent excavation in Kurdistan in northern Iraq unearthed a pot containing 60 tablets with another 30 tablets nearby.[26]

In the history of the book, clay tablets have one of the longest life spans. This technology was used from at least the late fourth millennium BCE through to the first century of the Common Era (CE). The youngest dated cuneiform tablet is from 75 CE.[27]

MODERN ADS FOR EARLY TECHNOLOGIES

Figure 1-5 Cuneiform tablet. Designed by Amelia Fontanel.

Cuneiform Tablets

Memory: Though scribes might write on all of the sides and edges of a tablet, overall the writing surfaces are still pretty small. It is perhaps akin to a page of printed text or the number of characters in a page written out in a word processing program. What would be the memory of such a document if it were digital? 10–50k? The transcription of the tablet shown in this ad requires roughly 16k of memory.

Readable/writable: In the case of a cuneiform tablet, the answer is yes. As we have seen, clay tablets were dried but not usually fully hardened. This allowed scribes to make the clay reusable by adding water to the clay, or by soaking the tablet and completely recycling it.

Durability: Once a cuneiform tablet hardens, it becomes quite durable. Surviving examples demonstrate that its rate of decay is quite slow, so if the tablet has not been damaged or destroyed by a human, it could easily last thousands of years. Fire, often an enemy to books, sometimes has a stabilizing effect on clay tablets, baking them into long-lasting rocks.

Security: Yes, a protective clay envelope can be wrapped around the tablet to secure its contents.

Access: On clay tablets, access is random, meaning the reader has access to any part of the text at any time by turning the tablet to one of its sides or edges. Random access stands in contrast to linear access, in which the reader has to move the device forward or backward sequentially to arrive at the information for which they are looking. Think, for example, of rewinding an audio cassette tape or fast-forwarding a VHS tape.

Cost: In the case of cuneiform clay tablets, the cost is very low—just one $. Clay, a combination of earthly materials such as stone and dirt, is a natural resource that is readily found in most areas of the world. Clay is fairly simple to process for use, and there is no real cost in the preparation of the tablet for writing.

Return to Tablet Culture

The cuneiform tablet was a robust reading and writing technology that lasted over three millennia. It introduced aspects of the book that influence various media that followed, and indeed continue today, for example, ruled pages, envelopes, and colophons. Cuneiform tablets also introduced the format of a handheld, reusable tablet, the contents of which could be secured. More than 5,000 years later, we have returned to a tablet culture. Today's owners of tablets and smartphones expect many of the same features from their devices. The materials used to create tablets have changed dramatically, and the uses of tablets have greatly expanded, yet at their core, modern tablets used almost ceaselessly throughout our day are a technology first conceived in ancient Mesopotamia.

FURTHER READING

Casson, Lionel. *Libraries in the Ancient World.* New Haven, CT: Yale University Press, 2001.

Charpin, Dominique. *Reading and Writing in Babylon.* Cambridge, MA: Harvard University Press, 2010.

Collon, Dominique. *Mesopotamia.* http://www.bbc.co.uk/history/ancient/cultures/mesopotamia_gallery.shtml.

Finkel, Irving, and Jonathan Taylor. *Cuneiform.* Los Angeles: The J. Paul Getty Museum, 2015.

Oxford Handbook of Cuneiform Culture. Edited by Karen Radner and Eleanor Robson. Oxford; New York: Oxford University Press, 2011.

Robson, Eleanor. "The Clay Tablet Book in Sumer, Assyria, and Babylonia." In *A Companion to the History of the Book*, edited by Simon Eliot and Jonathan Rose, 67–83. Malden, MA: Blackwell, 2007.

FURTHER TEACHING RESOURCE

Horry, Ruth A. "Downloadable Resources for Teaching and Events." *Nimrud: Materialities of Assyrian Knowledge Production.* The Nimrud Project at Oracc.org, 2015. http://oracc.iaas.upenn.edu/nimrud/abouttheproject/eventsresources.

PAPYRUS ROLLS

The clay tablet was not the only ancient writing and reading technology to take shape from natural resources harvested from riverbanks. Along the Nile River in Egypt grew tall tufted stalks of papyrus. As John Gaudet demonstrates in *Papyrus: The Plant That Changed the World*, papyrus was *the* vital resource of ancient Egypt, a civilization that thrived along the Nile River and Delta from the fourth millennium to the first century BCE. Papyrus could be used to make boats, ropes, and houses.[28] Heaven was imagined as a field of papyrus.[29] Papyrus was also the first material used to make paper. As Roemer notes, "The oldest known papyrus roll was found in the tomb of Hemaka in Saqqara, and dates to the 1st dynasty, around 2900 BC."[30] So it is safe to date the manufacture of papyrus paper to approximately 3000 BCE.[31]

Today we might think of paper as being writing material that is made from wood pulp. But wood-pulp paper was not invented until the 19th century (see Chapter Three). More generally, paper is a writing surface made from a great many different substrates. The first definition for paper given in the *Oxford English Dictionary* is helpful.

> Material in the form of thin, flexible sheets used for writing, printing, or drawing on, or for wrapping, covering, etc., usually made from wood pulp which is dried, pressed, and (generally) bleached.[32]

Making papyrus sheets was relatively easy and certainly inexpensive.[33] Stalks of papyrus, abundant at this time in Egypt, were gathered. The stalks, which could grow to a height of 4.5 meters (15 feet), were cut into shorter pieces, and then sliced into thin strips of about 25–38 cm (10–15 inches). These strips were laid flat side-by-side either vertically or horizontally to create one layer. A second layer of strips was laid flat side-by-side perpendicularly on top of the first.[34] Note that the strips are not woven together, but rather just laid perpendicularly on top of each other. The two layers of strips were then pressed together. This pressure releases the natural juices of the plant, which served as an adhesive that binds the layers together in one sheet.[35] The sheet was then dried.

The result was a flat writing surface—paper made from papyrus. For an illustrated step-by-step description of how to make a papyrus sheet, see this helpful blog post, "Making Papyrus in the Conservation Lab," by Caitlin Jenkins from the conservation lab of the Brooklyn Museum: https://www.brooklynmuseum.org/community/blogosphere/2010/07/08 /making-papyrus-in-the-conservation-lab.

Because the sheets were made from two perpendicular layers, there are two sides to papyrus—the recto and verso (these same terms will also be used later for terminology related to the codex book). The recto is the side where the papyrus grain runs horizontally. The verso is the side where the grain runs vertically. Typically, text was only written on the recto or horizontal surface. In fact, the horizontal grain of the papyrus created natural guidelines for the scribe—a kind of ancient ruled paper.[36] The recto side of the papyrus surface was prepared for writing by being smoothed with a pumice stone, shell, or other material.[37]

Papyrus was not sold in single sheets, but in longer rolls or scrolls. In *A Brief History of the Book*, we will be using the term "roll." Egypt produced papyrus sheets and exported them to areas throughout the Mediterranean, supplying civilizations such as Greece and the Roman Empire with paper.[38] To produce these rolls, about 20 individual sheets were glued together end-to-end using a wheat flour paste—the edge of the left sheet overlapping the right.[39] Papyrus rolls typically measured about 30 cm (12 inches) in height.[40] The length could vary depending on how many sheets were glued together. A normal-sized roll might measure about 6 meters (20 feet). That said, surviving examples measure as long as 30 meters (98 feet). As Roemer notes, in these cases they are most likely ritualistic rolls found in tombs, not rolls meant for reading.[41]

Writing on Papyrus

Figure 1-6 is a modern depiction of making and using papyrus painted by the artist Robert Thom around 1966.[42] This painting is a part of a series called *Communications Through the Ages*, commissioned by the Kimberly-Clark Company and donated to the Cary Graphic Arts Collection in 1975. Visible in the scene are the stalks of papyrus being harvested and papyrus strips being cut, laid out, flattened, and pressed. In the foreground, a scribe sits with a papyrus roll unrolled in his lap. In his right hand he holds a reed brush or pen. In his left hand he holds the edge of the roll and a palette of both black and red inks.

The black ink used to write on papyrus was made from a mixture of carbon and gum arabic, usually formed into a cake. Water was applied to the mixture until it was the right consistency and color for writing.[43] Red ink was made from the pigment iron oxide.[44] When the scribe wrote in red ink, it usually denoted significant parts of the text. Using red ink to highlight text is, of course, a design feature that can also be found in later books, from medieval European manuscripts to modern printing.

Figure 1-6   Robert A. Thom, *Papyrus and Pictography*, oil on canvas, 36 × 48 inches, Kimberly Clark Graphic Communications Through the Ages Series, c. 1966. RIT Cary Graphic Arts Collection.

The writing instrument used by the Egyptians was a brush made by trimming the end of a reed into a point and fraying or loosening its end. This created a tool that is similar to that of a modern brush. Later, the writing instrument used in Greece and Rome was a reed pen. Here a reed was cut so that it had a split nib at its end for holding and applying ink. A reed pen is similar to the quill used in the medieval period in Europe.[45] The text ran horizontally across the surface of the roll and in columns.

Reuse and Storage

Although scribes normally wrote on the recto side of the roll, it is not uncommon to find surviving rolls that have text on both the recto and verso sides. In these cases, it is likely that a scribe had reused a roll for a new text.[46] Reusing material is a common theme in the history of the book. Just as a clay tablet might be resoaked in water and reused when its text grew obsolete, so too might a parchment roll be reused. Rather than discard the roll and purchase new papyrus, it might be more economical to use its blank verso side as a writing surface. Evidence also suggests that papyrus rolls could be palimpsested; that is, the original text

Figure 1-7 "A Roman taking down a roll from its place in a library." John Willis Clark, *The Care of Books: An Essay on the Development of Libraries and their Fittings, from the Earliest Times to the End of the Eighteenth Century* (Cambridge, University Press, 1901), Figure II, p 35.

was erased and a new text was overwritten in its place. In the case of papyrus, the writing could be washed off with a "sponge or cloth."[47] Palimpsests are later an important aspect of codices made from parchment (see Chapter Two).

Papyrus rolls were not only a reusable technology, but also portable and easy to store. Rolled papyrus sheets would be stored on shelves, sometimes in pigeonhole-like compartments. Figure 1-7, depicts shelves of rolls in a Roman library. The triangle pieces hanging off the ends of most of the rolls are pasted-on tabs called sillyboi.[48] These tabs provided information about each roll such as the author and title of the work, thus facilitating identification and retrieval, whether on a shelf or stored upright in a cylindrical container called a capsa.[49] Otherwise such information would be typically found at the end of the text of the roll, not unlike the colophon at the end of a clay tablet.[50]

Papyrus rolls are a contemporary technology to cuneiform tablets and unsurprisingly were used in cultures that had similar literacy rates. Scholars estimate that about 1 percent of the population of Egypt would have been able to read or write.[51]

EXAMPLES FROM THE CARY COLLECTION

In ancient Egypt, one of the most common texts found written on papyrus rolls was the *Egyptian Book of the Dead*—the modern colloquial title for what at the time would have been called "Spells for Going Forth by Day."[52] This collection of texts would be buried with the deceased so that it might serve as a guide through the afterlife. The Cary Collection holds two fragments of ancient Egyptian papyrus rolls. The text of both is from the *Book of the Dead*. The first fragment (figure 1-8) dates to c. 1500 BCE and measures roughly 4.625 × 2 inches (11.9 × 5 cm). The script here is hieroglyphic—a pictorial system of writing used in Egypt. The second fragment (figure 1-9) dates to c. 323–30 BCE and measures 14.1875 × 4.875 (36 × 12.6 cm).[53] This script is hieratic, a shorthand form of writing that developed alongside of hieroglyphic writing.[54]

Figure 1-8 Fragment of the *Book of the Dead*, Egypt, c. 1500 BCE. RIT Cary Graphic Arts Collection. Photograph by Elizabeth Lamark.

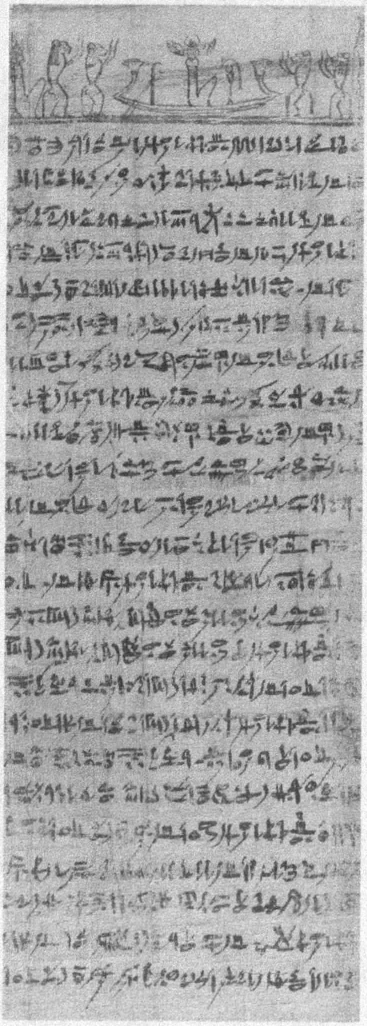

Figure 1-9 Fragment of the *Book of the Dead*, Egypt, c. 323–30 BCE. RIT Cary Graphic Arts Collection. Photograph by Elizabeth Lamark.

Parchment Rolls

Rolls could be made from material other than papyrus. Beginning in the final two centuries BCE, parchment came into use for writing.[55] Parchment is a writing surface made from the skins of animals—typically cows, sheep, or goats. In Chapter Two, the production of parchment will be described in greater detail. For now, it is worth noting that the skins of animals could be harvested, stretched, and scraped into a large, durable sheet. From the late ancient world through the European middle ages (c. 500–1400), parchment became the most-used writing surface. One of the chief reasons for this is that parchment is made from animal skins—a natural resource available in nearly every geographical location. This stands in contrast to papyrus, which was grown regionally in the Nile River Valley. Parchment is relatively costly in that, in order to make it, animals must be slaughtered and carefully processed, which takes time (and is actually quite nasty).

Parchment is one of the most robust and serviceable natural resources for writing. Roberts and Skeat go as far as writing that good quality

EXAMPLE FROM THE CARY COLLECTION

Figure 1-10 is an eighth-century parchment roll preserved at the Cary Collection. It is relatively small, with a height measuring 2.5 inches wide and 103 inches long (6.35 × 264.16 cm). The text is the Book of Esther in Hebrew. This is an important text in the Hebrew Bible as well as the Christian Old Testament. By the

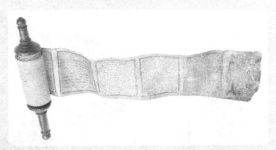

Figure 1-10 Book of Esther, 701–800 CE. RIT Cary Graphic Arts Collection. Photograph by Elizabeth Lamark.

eighth century, the codex was the most often used format for the written word in Europe; nevertheless, it is not surprising to see this text as a roll even during this period. The roll format has been and still survives as the writing medium used for Jewish texts. The history of the book is often intertwined with the history of religion. Different formats are often indicative or emblematic of different religions.

parchment is "the finest writing material ever devised by man. It is immensely strong, remains flexible indefinitely under normal conditions, does not deteriorate with age, and possesses a smooth, even surface for the finest writing and illumination."[56] Sheets of parchment could be sewn together in a roll; they could also be folded into pages of a codex book.

The surface of parchment is quite tough. In fact, text written on parchment is able to be scraped off or erased, making parchment a readable/writable material. Moreover, parchment is a reusable service. In fact, as we will see in Chapter Two, parchment documents can be palimpsested—that is, completely erased and overwritten. Parchment's pervasiveness did not happen quickly. The craft of preparing parchment needed time to develop—being more complicated in some ways than making cuneiform tablets or papyrus paper. A great many years would be necessary to refine the production and use of parchment for paper.

MODERN ADS FOR EARLY TECHNOLOGIES

Figure 1-11   Scroll. Designed by Amelia Fontanel.

Papyrus and Parchment Rolls

Memory: Rolls of any material hold a great deal of information and can be expanded simply by connecting more and more sheets.

Readable/writable: Text found on both papyrus and parchment can be erased and overwritten, though this seems a much more common feature for parchment.

Durability: Papyrus and parchment are both strong substrates. Depending on the conditions that rolls are kept in, and what natural disasters or human events they have had to endure, rolls of both materials can survive for thousands of years. Parchment is especially durable.

Security: The format of a roll provides a natural form of security. The text is typically written on one surface—the recto side. As the papyrus or parchment is rolled, the outside verso side serves as a protective layer.

Access: Rolls provide linear access. To get to certain specific parts of the text, the reader has to scroll either forward or backward.

Cost: Papyrus = $$. The production of papyrus was not expensive, and it was a relatively inexpensive writing resource for those dwelling in Egypt. Outside of that region, papyrus would have to be exported, and so the cost would increase. Parchment = $$$. Parchment is accessible wherever suitable animals are found. The cost of preparing animal skin as a writing surface is higher than using other found natural resources like clay, wax, and papyrus. The process, which will be explored in Chapter Two, took more time, labor, and resources.

FURTHER READING

Bagnall, Roger S., ed. *The Oxford Handbook of Papyrology*. Oxford; New York: Oxford University Press, 2009.

Gaudet, John J. *Papyrus: The Plant That Changed the World, from Ancient Egypt to Today's Water Wars*. New York: Pegasus Books, 2014.

Jenkins, Caitlin. "Making Papyrus in the Conservation Lab." Brooklyn Museum.org. July 2010. https://www.brooklynmuseum.org/community/blogosphere/2010/07/08/making-papyrus-in-the-conservation-lab (accessed February 3, 2020).

Parkinson, R. B. *Papyrus*. London: British Museum Press, 1995.

Roemer, Cornelia. "The Papyrus Roll in Egypt, Greece, and Rome." In *A Companion to the History of the Book*, edited by Simon Eliot and Jonathan Rose, 84–94. Malden, MA: Blackwell, 2007.

WAX TABLETS

The final ancient technology discussed in *A Brief History of the Book* may be best introduced with a riddle from the seventh century CE. Thus our time line temporarily jumps forward to Aldhelm, Abbot of Malmesbury, Bishop of Sherborne (d. 709/10). Aldhelm was a prolific writer who, in addition to writing religious works, composed riddles.[57] Among his collection of 100 riddles, or *Enigmata*, is one that describes a very important technology in the history of the book.

> Of honey-laden bees I first was born,
> But in the forest grew my outer coat;
> My shoes from tough hides came. An iron point
> In artful windings cuts a fair design,
> And leaves long, twisted furrows, like a plow. . . .[58]

Although Aldhelm writes in the seventh century, his riddle playfully provides clues that suggest a technology that dates back to approximately 1250 BCE—a wax tablet.[59] Wax tablets were a contemporary technology to cuneiform and papyrus rolls, and were in use in ancient Greece and Rome. What is helpful about Aldhelm's riddle is that he not only details what a wax tablet is made of, but also indicates how to use one. Figure 1-12 is a facsimile of a tablet that was once on display at The New York Times Museum of the Recorded Word, but is now used for teaching at the Cary Collection. With this image as our guide, let's sort out Aldhelm's riddle.

> *Of honey-laden bees I first was born.*

The riddle begins by identifying the beeswax that is used as the writing surface. The wax is usually dyed black or red.

> *But in the forest grew my outer coat.*

Its "outer coat" is wooded boards with carved recesses that hold the thin layers of beeswax. The outer sides of the first and last boards are not carved, and serve to protect the wax on the inner sides, much like a book's covers protect the pages within.

> *My shoes from tough hides came.*

This line, and its reference to "shoes," is a little more obscure. It refers to the leather cords that hold the boards together.

> *An iron point in artful windings cuts a fair design,*
> *And leaves long, twisted furrows, like a plow.*

The "iron point" is the stylus that is used to write on the beeswax. The process of writing is described in the riddle's final line. As the point of the stylus incises into the surface of the wax, it leaves grooves in its wake, just as the tracks of a plow leave furrows or trenches for planting. Note that the stylus in figure 1-12 is not only designed with a pointed tip for incising into the wax, but it also features a flat, tail fin-like end. This end is an eraser used for rubbing out existing text and preparing the wax surface for new writing. As with previous technologies, the material used to construct the wax tablet—beeswax, wood, rawhide, and metals such as bronze and iron—are all fairly common and accessible natural resources.

Figure 1-12 Wax Tablet, facsimile. RIT Cary Graphic Arts Collection.

Examples from Ancient Greece

The physical nature of wax tablets indicates how they were used. Their size is akin to a modern handheld tablet. As depictions in ancient art reveal, these tablets were held in one's hand while reading and writing. A famous image of a wax tablet is preserved on an early fifth-century Greek cup made by the artist Douris (fl. c. 500–c. 460 BCE), now held at the Staatliche Museen in Berlin.[60] The cup depicts a Greek school where a seated man is teaching a boy how to use a wax tablet. The man's set of tablets consists of three pieces of wood, thus likely providing four wax surfaces. The stylus he uses has both a pointed end for writing and a flattened end for erasing.

The use of a wax tablet in the context of education illustrates one of the principle functions of this technology. As Rouse and Rouse observe, "Wax was the medium in which all children formed their first letters and then learned how to write. From antiquity to the 16th century, the wax tablet was part of the furniture of the primary schoolroom and the principal hand-baggage of the elementary schoolchild."[61] The authors continue on to identify a second fundamental function: "The tablet was the medium on which ancient and medieval authors composed their texts, serving as the equivalent of the modern lined yellow pad or personal computer screen."[62] These ephemeral uses make the most of the wax tablet's reusability and portability. Wax tablets were not often the site of permanent records, but rather the medium for exercises, rough drafts, and note taking. The texts written on them would not be of any substantial length, as wax tablets tended to have a limited number of wooden leaves with wax surfaces. Roberts and Skeat note that "no specimen surviving from antiquity has more than ten."[63]

Texts written on tablets likely did not circulate at all, except perhaps if used for correspondence. This sort of technology speaks not to public dissemination of information, but rather to private use. The wax tablet was more of a personal, educational, or household device. The process of writing on a wax tablet was less formal as well. It was portable and could be written on with a stylus while standing up, as compared to writing on papyrus and later parchment, where one would need to be seated with easy access to an ink supply.[64]

Returning to the fifth-century Douris Greek cup, what might be striking to modern viewers about this image is how much the ancient wax tablet resembles our modern laptop computer. Although the man rests the tablet on his forearm, and not in his lap or on a table, the shape of the tablet, and how the man appears to be operating it, is uncannily familiar. Other ancient works of art depict wax tablets being used in a similar fashion. Evidently, wax tablets were not just for mere mortals. A Greek vase dating to c. 480 BCE preserved at the Staatliche Antikensammlungen, Munich, shows the goddess Athena standing and writing on a wax tablet.[65] Here, too, the tablet is held in one hand while the stylus is held in the other. In both examples, the wax tablets are opened horizontally like laptops. In this case, the text would have been "written in lines parallel to the long side of the tablet."[66]

Examples from Ancient Rome

Evidence from later images suggests that wax tablets were also handled vertically like printed or manuscript books. A painting from a wall fresco c. 55–79 CE survives from Pompeii, the Roman city that was buried when Mt. Vesuvius erupted in the year 79 CE. The painting, titled *Portrait of the So-Called Sappho* by modern scholars, depicts the bust of a young Roman woman.[67] In her left hand she holds a wax tablet consisting of four pieces of wood, likely giving her six wax writing surfaces (the two outer protective surfaces are likely not carved out for wax). The wooden leaves are bound together along the long edge with a ribbon, so that they can be opened and closed. In her right hand she holds a long, pointed metal stylus, which clearly has a flattened tail end that would have been used as an eraser. She rests the stylus near her lips in a pensive pose. Unlike the Greek examples mentioned above, the Roman woman positions her tablet vertically, in the same manner as those of you reading *A Brief History of the Book* in book form.[68] This painting survives in the National Archaeological Museum of Naples.

The nature and uses of the wax tablet are further exemplified in another first-century fresco from the Roman city of Pompeii now held in the National Archaeological Museum of Naples. This painting from c. 55–79 CE depicts a bakery owner named Terentius Neo and his wife. Each one holds a different writing technology. In Neo's wife's hands are a wax tablet and a stylus. Indeed, she rests the stylus near her lips in a pose similar to the contemporary *Portrait of the So-Called Sappho*. She also positions the tablets vertically, but facing outwardly so that viewers can see that the wax surfaces have been dyed black (an artistic choice for which modern historians are grateful). Terentius Neo holds in his right hand a roll likely made of papyrus. Hanging from one of the ends of the roll is a sillyboi, likely identifying the text's title. As Cornelia Roemer rightly notes, this painting

> tells a story not only about different writing materials, but also about the respective social roles of these materials. While the husband holds a papyrus roll, thus showing his literacy and noble education, his wife holds a wax tablet, presenting herself as a good housewife who keeps her records carefully.[69]

The roll and tablet held by Terentius Neo and his wife exemplify the differences between a technology meant for long-lasting works that might circulate beyond the household, and ephemeral works that were perhaps more domestic and did not circulate (https://www.museoarcheologiconapoli .it/en/room-and-sections-of-the-exhibition/frescoes).

The Longevity of Wax Tablets

Our discussion of wax tablets began with a seventh-century riddle from Aldhelm. That is more than 1,500 years after this technology first came into use. Yet wax tablets continued to be used well beyond even the age of Aldhelm. Two later literary references give evidence to this longevity.

Geoffrey Chaucer's *The Canterbury Tales* is a masterpiece of medieval English literature. In the poem, a diverse group of characters are on a pilgrimage from London to Canterbury. To entertain each other they tell tales. Whomever, in the judgement of Harry Bailly, host of the Tabard Inn, tells the "tales of best sentence and moost solas"[70] wins a free dinner at his inn. When it is the Summoner's turn, he tells a story of a corrupt friar in an effort to retaliate for the previous tale told by the Friar, which had unkind things to say about summoners. The Summoner describes a friar, who after preaching and begging in church, further begs food from the townsfolk. He records all who give him goods in a wax tablet made of ivory, but then erases the name after he leaves:

> His felawe hadde a staf tipped with horn,
> A paire of tables al of ivory,
> And a pointel polisshed fetisly,
> And wroot the names alway as he stood
> Of alle folk that yaf hem any good, . . .
> And whan that he was out at dore, anon
> He planed away the names everichon
> That he biforn hadde writen in his tables: (*Summoner's Tale,* 1740–1744, 1757–1759)[71]

Planing "away the names" of "everichon" or "everyone" inscribed in the tablet is illustrative of the act of using the back end of the stylus to flatten out and erase the text written in the wax. Chaucer penned *The Canterbury Tales* during roughly the last decade of the 14th century. This means that a technology begun in the second millennium BCE lasted through the medieval period in Europe.

By the 16th century, a modified version of the wax tablet had been developed. A mixture of gesso (plaster of Paris) and glue was applied to the surface of paper or parchment creating a coated surface that could be written on with a metal stylus of brass or copper. Writing was not done by digging into the surface, as with wax, but was more akin to writing on a chalkboard. Writing with a metal stylus left a visible deposit on the surface that could be wiped away with a little moisture.[72] This technology was most deeply studied at the Folger Shakespeare Library by Heather Wolfe, Peter Stallybrass, Roger Chartier, and J. Franklin Mowery. Their article, "Hamlet's Tablets and the Technologies of Writing in Renaissance England," begins with a passage from Shakespeare's *Hamlet*:

Remember thee?
Ay, thou poore ghost, while memory holds a seat
In this distracted globe. Remember thee?
Yea, from the table of my memory
I'll wipe away all trivial fond records,
All saws of books, all forms, all pressures past,
That youth and observation copied there,
And thy commandment all alone shall live
Within the book and volume of my brain
Unmixed with baser matter. (1.5.95–104)[73]

The metaphor of a "tabula rasa" (a clean or blank slate) was fairly common,[74] but Shakespeare expands on it. Hamlet uses a "table" (meaning tablet) as a metaphor for human memory—a "table of my memory" off of which he can "wipe" or erase memories that he once recorded. Shakespeare composed *Hamlet* in around 1600. Readable/writable writing tables or tablets like these continue to survive even beyond this time, though in decreasing numbers. By the 19th century, as paper became cheaper and more plentiful (and to some degree disposable with the advent of wood-pulp paper), reusable writing technologies such as tablets became increasingly obsolete. Then again, similar concepts persist in everything from chalkboards and whiteboards, to erasable digital tablets such as Boogie Board's eWriters.

The Wax Tablet and the Codex

The impact of the wax tablet extended well beyond the use of such devices. The wax tablet introduced one of the most important formats in the history of the book—the codex. Let's return to the images of Roman women from Pompeii holding tablets. At first glance, the tablets might look like books as we know them. Their size and shape, and the manner in which they are held, are familiar to modern readers. The construction of wax tablets is the early form of the codex, that is: leaves of some material bound along one edge, allowing random access to all of its surfaces. Fundamentally, wax tablets are books in the form with which we are familiar, but they are made of wood and wax, and bound with leather string or cloth. This is the codex format that will evolve into the form of the book that continues today.

MODERN ADS FOR EARLY TECHNOLOGIES

Figure 1-13   Wax Tablet. Designed by Amelia Fontanel.

Wax Tablets

Memory: If the average wax tablet consisted of three wooden leaves housing four wax writing surfaces, that is the equivalent of about four printed pages of text. Wax tablets are expandable. More wax surfaces can be added, though they do not go beyond 10 boards.

Readable/writable: Yes. The core function of a wax tablet is the ability to write and erase text.

Durability: Wax tablets should provide years of readable/writable use, but are not made for permanent records.

Security: The wooden leaves that hold the thin layer of wax also serve to protect the wax. The first and last wooden boards usually have wax only on the inside. Thus, these boards serve a protective function much like that of book covers.

Access: Random access is one of the most important features of the codex structure. By turning pages (leaves), readers have access to any part of the text at any time.

Cost: $$. Wax and wood are both inexpensive natural resources. The process of making a wax tablet is straightforward and inexpensive.

PALM LEAF MANUSCRIPTS: ANOTHER EARLY BOOK FORM

The palm leaf manuscript (or palm leaf book) was a handheld book format dating back to about the fifth century BCE in South and Southeast Asia.[75] As the name suggests, the writing surface for this book format was dried palm leaves. Palm leaves of about 19 inches long were cut in half and sanded flat.[76] The rectangular leaf might be ruled by snapping soot-covered string onto it, creating temporary horizontal lines.[77] A scribe then etched the text into the leaves using a metal stylus. This left blind recesses without any color. The scribe then rubbed ink across the leaf, filling the etched, recessed areas with ink. The remaining, excess ink was then rubbed off, leaving ink just in the now visible written content. Text was written on both sides of the palm leaf. When the writing was complete, the leaves were gathered in a stack to be bound. Two wooden boards, roughly the same size as the palm leaves, were placed below and on top of the stack. One or two holes were made through the boards and leaves. A long string was threaded in the hole(s), holding the leaves and boards together and facilitating reading the leaves by spreading them out. To secure the palm leaf book when it was not being read, the string was wrapped several times around the book. Figure 1-14 shows a an undated palm leaf fragment held at the Cary Collection resting beside a modern palm leaf book that is closed and wrapped.

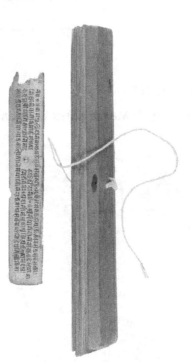

Figure 1-14 A modern palm leaf book and an undated fragment. RIT Cary Graphic Arts Collection.

FURTHER READING

Rouse, Richard H., and Mary A. Rouse. "Wax Tablets." *Language & Communication* 9, no. 2/3 (1989): 175–191.

Stallybrass, Peter, Roger Chartier, J. Franklin Mowery, and Heather Wolfe. "Hamlet's Tablets and the Technologies of Writing in Renaissance England." *Shakespeare Quarterly* 55, no. 4 (2004): 379–419.

ACTIVITIES

Activity 1: Making and Using a Cuneiform Tablet

Figure 1-15   A homemade clay tablet.

Objectives

Shaping clay into a handheld tablet, readers will make their own cuneiform tablets. Through writing exercises on the tablet, readers will get a sense of how to use a cuneiform tablet, while also learning how written language evolved from pictographs to symbolic characters.

Supplies

- Air-drying clay.
- 1 unsharpened three-sided pencil. Alternatively, a chopstick with a squared end may be used.
- 1 sharpened pencil.
- 1 bottle Mod Podge Waterbase Sealer, Glue and Finish (optional).

Instructions

1. Take a handful of clay into your hand and shape it into a square, rectangular, or circular tablet. The size can vary, but the tablet should fit comfortably in your hand. The tablet should be about ½ inch thick.

2. Hold the sharpened pencil in the hand with which you write. Hold the blank clay tablet in your other hand. Using figure 1-2 as a guide, inscribe the pictorial symbol for barley as it would have appeared c. 3100 BCE.

3. Now hold the unsharpened three-sided pencil or chopstick in your hand. Using figure 1-2 as a guide, inscribe the symbol for barley as it would have appeared c. 700 BCE.

4. Following figure 1-2, use the unsharpened three-sided pencil or chopstick to inscribe the numbers 1 to 5 into your tablet.

5. Leave your tablet for 72 hours to air dry.

6. To further stabilize your tablet, you may brush on a layer or two of Mod Podge.

Note to add: This exercise is inspired by several online resources, including: http://pages.mtu.edu/~scmarkve/2910Su11/WrSys/evolofcuneiform3100 -600BC.htm (removed but accessible through the Internet Archive's Wayback Machine).

Activity 2: Making Wax Tablets

Objectives

Readers will learn how wax tablets were made by producing one of their own. Once the tablets are complete, they can use them as a part of an experiential assignment.

There are number of ways to make wax tablets, each with its own level of difficulty. Instructions have been published or posted online for wax tablets made from material ranging from card-

Figure 1-16   A homemade wax tablet.

board to plywood.[78] Working with plywood requires woodworking tools that might not be accessible; cardboard might not create tablets that are authentic enough. This exercise takes a middle road and creates tablets using balsa wood. This wood achieves a more accurate look and is soft enough to cut with a utility knife.

Supplies

   1 pencil

   1 heavy-duty utility knife

   1 bottle of wood glue

   1 awl or drill with 11/64 bit

   1 sheet of balsa wood 3/16×3×36 inches

   1 sheet of balsa wood 1/8×3×36 inches

   1 roll of 1/8-inch suede leather lace

   1 candle-making pitcher or double boiler pot

   1 sauce pan

   1 bag beeswax pellets or small blocks of beeswax (blocks can be hard to cut—small blocks are recommended)

   1 packet of wooden styluses

   (optional) 1 bottle black or red dye, or black or red crayon

Instructions

Making the Wooden Tablets

1. Take a sheet of 3/16×3×36-inch balsa wood and measure 4.5 inches from one of its ends. Make a perpendicular line with a pencil. Use a utility knife to cut along the line, creating a piece of wood that is 4.5×3 inches. Note: Balsa wood is very easy to cut along the grain; however, cutting against the grain can be more difficult. Take your time. It sometimes helps to measure and mark both sides of the wood and alternate cutting from both sides.

2. Repeat step 1 using the 1/8×3×36-inch-thick balsa wood sheet.

3. Take the 1/8-thick piece of balsa wood and measure in 1/2 inch from all sides. Mark with a pencil.

4. Use a utility knife to cut along the lines. Remove the interior wood so that you are left with a 1/2-inch wooden frame.

5. Carefully glue the 1/2-inch frame onto the 3/16-inch piece. Place a weight or heavy book on top and let dry for 30 minutes to an hour.

6. Repeat steps 1 through 5 to create a second tablet.

Drilling Holes for the Leather Ties

1. Using an 11/64 bit, drill matching holes in the upper and lower corners of one side of the tablet. Balsa wood can splinter when drilled, so use care. Once the holes are drilled, you may insert the tip of a sharpened pencil and turn it to smooth out the holes.

Adding the Wax

1. Place beeswax into a candle-making pitcher. The amount of wax depends on how many tablets you plan to make.
2. Boil water in a saucepan and reduce to a simmer.
3. Carefully insert the candle-making pitcher into the saucepan and onto the simmering water.
4. Stir the wax occasionally as it melts. If you are using a black or red crayon to color the wax, you can add it now.
5. When the wax is fully melted, turn off the heat and carefully remove the pitcher from the saucepan. If you are adding dye to color the wax, do so after you turn off the heat. Add and stir in the dye until satisfied with the color.
6. Carefully pour the hot wax into each tablet until it reaches the rim of the recess.
7. Do not move tablets until wax is fully cooled.

Tying the Tablets Together

1. Cut two 6-inch laces from roll of suede leather lace.
2. Insert laces into upper and lower holes, and tie the tablets together along the edge.

The Wooden Stylus

1. Wooden styluses can often be purchased at craft stores or online. Some styluses come with a flattened end. If they do not have a flattened end, you can carefully flatten the end using a knife.

Note: If you would rather not make your own wax tablets, there are contemporary makers found on Etsy who can supply you with some.

ASSIGNMENTS

Assignment 1

Write a page reflecting on the experience of making and writing on a clay tablet. How is handling a clay tablet similar to handling a modern tablet? Consider the differences in writing the symbol for barley in 3100 BCE versus c. 700 BCE.

Assignment 2

Complete the assignment "Mastering Graffiti on a Palm" (see Chapter Four). Write a page reflecting on your experiences using both your cuneiform tablet and Palm device. How are these handheld devices similar or dissimilar?

Assignment 3

Now that readers have made wax tablets and styluses, they need to use them. Carry your tablet with you for a week, just as you might carry your smartphone or tablet. At the end of the week, write a brief journal detailing your use of the tablet. What did you use it for? What did you find helpful or frustrating? Why did this technology last for so very long? How do current devices relate to the wax tablet?

NOTES

1. Irving Finkel and Jonathan Taylor, *Cuneiform* (Los Angeles: The J. Paul Getty Museum, 2015), 6.

2. Jonathan Taylor, "Tablets as Artefacts, Scribes as Artisans," in *Oxford Handbook of Cuneiform Cultures,* ed. Karen Radner and Eleanor Robson (Oxford; New York: Oxford University Press, 2011), 12.

3. Eleanor Robson, "The Clay Tablet Book in Sumer, Assyria, and Babylonia," in *A Companion to the History of the Book*, ed. Simon Eliot and Jonathan Rose (Malden, MA: Blackwell, 2007), 67; Martyn Lyons, *Books: A Living History* (Los Angeles: J. Paul Getty Museum, 2011), 16.

4. Finkel and Taylor, *Cuneiform,* 76.

5. For illustrations showing how to make a reed stylus, see http://cdli .ox.ac.uk/wiki/doku.php?id=cuneiform_writing_techniques and https:// cdli.ucla.edu/pubs/cdln/php/single.php?id=65.

6. Taylor, "Tablets," 15.

7. Ibid.

8. Ibid., 13.

9. Finkel and Taylor, *Cuneiform,* 75.

10. Marcel Sigrist, *Documents from Tablet Collections in Rochester New York* (Bethesda, MD: CDL Press, 1991), 11, 108. For the description of this tablet in the *Cuneiform Digital Library Initiative*, see https://cdli .ucla.edu/search/archival_view.php?ObjectID=P128277.

11. Lionel Casson, *Libraries in the Ancient World* (New Haven, CT: Yale University Press, 2001), 2.

12. Robson, "Clay Tablet," 68.

13. Ibid., 73.

14. "colophon, n.," OED Online, December 2018, Oxford University Press. http://www.oed.com.ezproxy.rit.edu/view/Entry/36552?rskey=od7jyu&result =2&isAdvanced=false (accessed December 3, 2018).

15. Finkel and Taylor, *Cuneiform,* 54.

16. Robson, "Clay Tablet," 74.

17. Casson, *Libraries,* 14; Denis J. Murphy, *People, Plants, and Genes: The Story of Crops and Humanity* (Oxford; New York: Oxford University Press, 2007), 224.

18. Dominique Charpin, *Reading and Writing in Babylon* (Cambridge, MA: Harvard University Press, 2010), 212.

19. Xenophon, *Cyrupaedia: The Institution and Life of Cyrus, the First of That Name, King of Persians* (London: Printed by J. L. [i.e. John Legate] for Robert Allot . . . 1632).

20. Charpin, *Reading and Writing,* 72.

21. Taylor, "Tablets," 20.

22. Finkel and Taylor, *Cuneiform,* 60.

23. Ibid., 32. For a revaluation of notions of literacy in Mesopotamia, see Charpin, *Reading and Writing,* 53–67

24. Casson, *Libraries,* 2.

25. Finkel and Taylor, *Cuneiform,* 37; Robson, "Clay Tablet," 70.

26. Rachel Riederer, "Archaeologists Discover Trove of Cuneiform Tablets in Northern Iraq," Smithsonian.com, October 24, 2017. https:// www.smithsonianmag.com/smart-news/archaeologists-cuneiform-tablets -northern-iraq-180966923.

27. Robson, "Clay Tablet," 69.

28. John J. Gaudet, *Papyrus: The Plant That Changed the World, from Ancient Egypt to Today's Water Wars* (New York: Pegasus Books, 2014), 28–29, 46.

29. Ibid., 44.

30. Cornelia Roemer, "The Papyrus Roll in Egypt, Greece, and Rome," in *A Companion to the History of the Book*, ed. Simon Eliot and Jonathan Rose (Malden, MA: Blackwell, 2007), 84.

31. Casson, *Libraries,* 25; Roemer, "Papyrus Roll," 84.

32. "paper, n. and adj.," OED Online, June 2018, Oxford University Press. http://www.oed.com.ezproxy.rit.edu/view/Entry/137122?rskey=R1iJOM& result=1&isAdvanced=false (accessed August 11, 2018).

33. Gaudet, *Papyrus*, 48.

34. There has been scholarly discussion about whether and how the papyrus strips overlapped each other. See Adam Bülow-Jacobsen, "Writing Materials in the Ancient World," in *The Oxford Handbook of Papyrology*, ed. Roger S. Bagnall (Oxford; New York: Oxford University Press, 2009), 8–11.

35. Roemer, "Papyrus Roll," 85.

36. Penelope Wilson, *Hieroglyphs: A Very Short Introduction* (Oxford; New York: Oxford University Press, 2004), 72.

37. Roemer, 85.

38. Lyons, 21; Roemer, 84; Gaudet, 46; Casson, 25.

39. Casson, 25; Bülow-Jacobsen, 19.

40. Roemer, 86.

41. Ibid. See also Lyons, 21.

42. Robert A. Thom, *Papyrus and Pictography*, oil on canvas, Kimberly Clark Graphic Communications through the Ages Series, c. 1960.

43. Wilson, 72.

44. Rachel Danzing, "Pigments and Inks Typically Used on Papyrus," September 22, 2010. https://www.brooklynmuseum.org/community/blogo sphere/2010/09/22/pigments-and-inks-typically-used-on-papyrus.

45. Bülow-Jacobsen, "Writing Materials," 3; Roemer, "Papyrus Roll," 87. See also https://sites.dartmouth.edu/ancientbooks/2016/05/23/the-writing -instrument-the-reed-and-quill-and-ink.

46. Bülow-Jacobsen, "Writing Materials," 21.

47. Colin H. Roberts and T. C. Skeat, *The Birth of the Codex* (London; New York: Published for the British Academy by the Oxford University Press, 1983), 17.

48. Roemer, "Papyrus Roll," 86. For illustrations of sillyboi, see the section "Book Titles and Tags" of http://www.papyrology.ox.ac.uk/POxy /VExhibition/scribes_scholars/scribes_contents.html.

49. For a dramatic example of a capsa, see the one depicted at the feet of the Statue of Sophocles in the Lateran Museum in Rome: https://commons

.wikimedia.org/wiki/Category:Statue_of_Sophocles_in_the_Lateran
Museum(Rome).

50. Roemer, "Papyrus Roll," 86.

51. Lyons, 15; Roemer, 89; Wilson, 50.

52. Stephen E. Thompson, "Egyptian Book of the Dead: Document Analysis ca. 1569–1315 BCE," in *Milestone Documents of World Religions* (Salem Press, 2017). https://ezproxy.rit.edu/login?url=https://search.credoreference.com/content/entry/greymdwr/egyptian_book_of_the_dead_document_analysis_ca_1569_1315_bce/0?institutionId=3255.

53. Many thanks to Dr. Ann-Katrin Gill of University College Oxford for her help in dating this fragment.

54. Wilson, *Hieroglyphs*, 18.

55. Roberts and Skeat, *Birth,* 6, 15.

56. Ibid., 8.

57. Lapidge, Michael. 2004 "Aldhelm [St Aldhelm] (d. 709/10), Abbot of Malmesbury, Bishop of Sherborne, and Scholar," *Oxford Dictionary of National Biography,* December 24, 2018. http://www.oxforddnb.com/view/10.1093/ref:odnb/9780198614128.001.0001/odnb-9780198614128-e-308.

58. Saint Aldhelm, *The Riddles of Aldhelm. Text and Verse Translation with Notes by James Hall Pitman* (Hamden, CT: Archon Books, 1970), 18–19; Richard H. Rouse and Mary A. Rouse, "Wax Tablets," *Language & Communication* 9, no. 2/3 (1989): 175; Greg Priest-Dorman and Carolyn Priest-Dorman, "Making and Using Waxed Tablets," https://www.cs.vassar.edu/~capriest/tablets.html.

59. An early example of wax tablets from the Late Bronze Age (1250–1000 BCE) was discovered during an archaeological recovery of an ancient shipwreck near Turkey. See Robert Payton, "The Ulu Burun Writing-Board Set," *Anatolian Studies* 41 (1991): 99–106.

60. http://www.smb-digital.de/eMuseumPlus?service=ExternalInterface&module=collection&objectId=686551&viewType=detailView https://www.bpk-bildagentur.de/shop.

61. Rouse and Rouse, "Wax Tablets," 175.

62. Ibid.

63. Roberts and Skeat, *Birth*, 12.

64. Rouse and Rouse, 178.

65. https://www.theoi.com/Gallery/K8.4.html.

66. Bülow-Jacobsen, 12.

67. https://www.museoarcheologiconapoli.it/en/room-and-sections-of-the-exhibition/frescoes.

68. For medieval illustration of writers using wax tablets, see Rouse and Rouse 181 and 182.

69. Roemer, "Papyrus Roll," 85; Casson, *Libraries*, 126.

70. Geoffrey Chaucer et al., *The Norton Chaucer* (New York: Norton, 2019), 94.

71. Ibid., 241.

72. Stallybrass, Peter, Roger Chartier, J. Franklin Mowery, and Heather Wolfe, "Hamlet's Tablets and the Technologies of Writing in Renaissance England," *Shakespeare Quarterly* 55, no. 4 (2004): 388, 408.

73. William Shakespeare et al., *2015. The Norton Shakespeare* (New York: Norton, 1997), 1686.

74. "tabula, n.," OED Online, December 2018, Oxford University Press. http://www.oed.com.ezproxy.rit.edu/view/Entry/196842?redirectedFrom =tabula+rasa (accessed January 12, 2019).

75. Zhixin Shi, Srirangaraj Setlur, and Venu Govindaraju, "Digital Enhancement of Palm Leaf Manuscript Images Using Normalization Techniques" (PDF). Amherst, USA: SUNY at Buffalo.

76. Montgomery Schuyler, "Notes on the Making of Palm-Leaf Manuscripts in Siam," *Journal of the American Oriental Society* 29 (1908): 282.

77. Ibid.

78. See Kathryn Murdock, "Make Your Own Wax Tablet and Stylus," *Calliope* 9, no. 3 (November 1998) and *Everyday Archaeology: Roman Wax Tablet*, https://www.youtube.com/watch?v=L-lnCoEHuXs&t=117s.

TWO

Early Printing and
Medieval Manuscripts

PAPER AND WOODBLOCK PRINTING

One of the themes in the history of the book thus far is the use of natural resources to create writing surfaces. Examples include clay, wax, and papyrus. Each resource has its own characteristics, and each influenced the way humans wrote on their surfaces.

In the early second century of the Common Era (CE), paper was invented in China. This is undoubtedly one of the most important developments in the history of writing. For modern readers, paper is ubiquitous; it is cheap and disposable. This is due primarily to the development of wood-pulp paper in the mid-19th century. Before then, paper was a more valued resource. Tradition has it that Cai Lun invented paper in China in 105 CE, using materials like silk, hemp, rags, or tree bark.[1] Natural resources such as these were soaked in water until their fibers broke down. This created the liquid pulp. A mesh screen was dipped into a vat of pulp. The pulp spread across the screen and, when dried, created a sheet a paper. As the eminent American paper historian Dard Hunter more eloquently describes it:

> To be classed as true paper the thin sheets must be made from fibre that has been macerated until each individual filament is a separate unit; the fibres intermixed with water, and by the use of a sieve-like screen, the fibres lifted from the water in the form of a thin stratum, the water draining through the small openings of the screen, leaving

a sheet of matted fibre upon the screen's surface. This thin layer of intertwined fiber is paper. This was the manner in which the Chinese eunuch Ts'ai Lun formed the first paper . . .[2]

By 105 CE, writing in China had already been practiced for some time. Chinese writing dates to the middle of the second millennium BCE, and can be found on a variety of substrates, including tortoise shells, animal bones, bamboo strips (c. 600 BCE), and silk (c. 475 BCE).[3] An early book form called the jiance or jiandu dates to the fourth century BCE in China. This early structure consisted of thin strips of bamboo or wood, tethered vertically side-by-side with cord.[4] This created a writing surface. Ink characters were then brushed onto the strips.

The invention of paper, however, made possible the invention of the first form of relief printing—woodblock printing. In this process, conceived in China around the seventh century, text and image were carved in reverse into a block of wood.[5] Ink was then applied to the surface of the engraved wood. Figure 2-1 is a detail of a woodblock engraving from the Cary Collection. Measuring 23.75×6.25 inches (60.3×15.8 cm), this is a much later Japanese example used for a book titled *Kaso Zukai* printed in Edo in 1798. Next to it is the print that the woodblock produces. A translation of the text reveals that it is essentially a feng shui manual advising on the proper arrangement of one's home.[6]

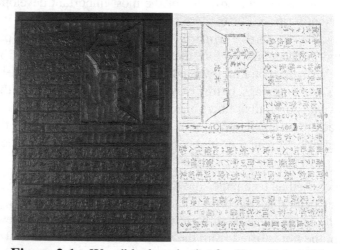

Figure 2-1   Woodblock and print for *Kaso Zukai*, Edo Japan, c. 1798. RIT Cary Graphic Arts Collection.

Woodblock printing was a relief printing process, so the ink rested on the raised surfaces or peaks of the carved block, not in the valleys created by carving. A piece of paper was placed on the inked block. The paper and block were not put into a press, but rather the text and image of the inked block were transferred onto paper through pressure printing. A hand-held, disk-shaped tool called a baren was used to press or rub the paper against the block, creating a right-reading impression. Due to this need to press or rub, woodblock printing was usually done on only one side of the paper; otherwise the process would mar what had been previously printed. Woodblock printing is still an art form. Today, artists sometimes also use a similar process, carving into a linoleum block and pressure printing the text or image.

AN EXAMPLE FROM THE CARY COLLECTION

Figure 2-2 *Hyakumanto Darani*, Japan, c. 770 CE. RIT Cary Graphic Arts Collection. Photograph by Elizabeth Lamark.

Woodblock printing spread to Japan and Korea by at least the mid-eighth century.[7] It is from this era in Japan that we find one of the earliest known texts most likely printed from a woodblock.[8] Figure 2-2 is a copy of the *Hyakumanto Darani* roll that is preserved in the Cary Collection. It measures 2.25 inches (5.7 cm) wide. Due to its condition it is unable to be unrolled. Judging from other surviving copies, it likely measures about 17.5 inches (45 cm) long. Its history provides a fascinating look into what was perhaps the first mass-produced book. In about 764 CE, there was a failed rebellion against the Japanese Empress Shotoku. Sometime afterward, the empress commanded the printing of more than 100,000 copies of a Buddhist invocation or dharani. The rolls were housed in wooden, pagoda-shaped receptacles and delivered to temples all across the country.[9] For these reasons, the publication is sometimes referred to as the One Million Pagodas. The exact number of copies produced is unknown, though the large number of surviving copies suggests that the print run was indeed quite sizable. The Cary Collection's copy of the *Hyakumanto Darani* roll no longer has its original pagoda housing, but many of the pagodas still survive.[10]

The *Hyakumanto Darani* was one of the very first books, or substantial texts, printed on paper, yet it is important to note that these rolls were not printed for the purpose of reading. As Peter Kornicki notes,

> Although indubitably the first instance of mass-production printing in the world, these invocations are evidence not of the printing of texts for the benefit of readers but of printing as a ritual act, for the point was simply the multiple production of copies of the text. They were not for reading or even distribution: the pagodas with their contents were stored in temples and not examined until the 19th century.[11]

Evidence suggests that there may have been at least one earlier example of woodblock printing prior to the *Hyakumanto Darani*. As Kornicki writes, "in 1966 a similar printed dharani was found in a stone pagoda at the Pulguska temple in Kyongju, Korea. Although it is not dated and there is no documentary record of the printing, it is thought to date to sometime before 751."[12] This text, the *Pure Light Dharani Sutra*, was printed from 12 woodblocks on paper made of mulberry bark. This surviving text might be "the earliest printed specimen in the world."[13]

Diamond Sutra

Perhaps the most famous example of an early book printed on paper using woodblocks is the *Diamond Sutra* of 868 CE. Scholars point to this roll as the first known dated printed book.[14] Printed in China, the text is the Jin-gang Jing or "Dialog with the Buddha." The name *Diamond Sutra* is taken from a passage in the text. When the Buddha is asked what the Sutra should be called, he replies "call it 'The Diamond of Transcendent Wisdom' because its teaching will cut like a diamond blade through worldly illusion to illuminate what is real and everlasting."[15] Measuring over 5 meters long, the *Diamond Sutra* is a large roll printed with woodblocks on hemp and mulberry-based paper. It is currently held at the British Library.

It is important to pause for a moment to observe that these important early printed texts—the *Hyakumanto Darani*, the *Pure Light Dharani*

Sutra, and the *Diamond Sutra*—are Buddhist texts. The importance of religious texts in the history of the book can never be understated. In India, China, Korea, and Japan, Buddhism helped advance the book. These early printed texts are also rolls. This format endured to some degree in the first millennia of the Common Era, but times were changing. As J. S. Edgren argues, one of the great advancements in the history of the book was the understanding "that the leaves of a book need not be attached continuously."[16] This advancement—the rise of the codex—took hold in the third and fourth centuries CE and was propelled by the spread of Christianity in the West.

The Roll vs. Codex

The fourth century was a time of significant change in the history of the book. It was the period in which the codex become the format of choice for books in the Middle East and Europe. As demonstrated in Chapter One with wax tablets, a codex may be described as leaves of some substrate bound together along the long edge. As Roberts and Skeat note, by about 300 CE, the codex form had "achieved parity with the roll."[17] But by the end of the fourth century the codex had overtaken the roll.

There are a number of possible reasons for this change. Most of the reasons speak to how practical and user-friendly the codex is as a format. For example, a scribe could write on both sides of the pages of a codex (and later both sides would be printed on). Writing on rolls tended to be found only on the recto side. In this way, codices could hold more information. Due to this greater capacity, the codex had "the ability to bring together within two covers texts which had hitherto circulated separately."[18]

The spread of the codex was also spurred by religious changes. In the fourth century CE, Christianity was spreading through the Roman Empire. As Christianity continued to spread, the words of its Old and New Testaments were circulated primarily in codices. As Peter Stallybrass has observed,

> Christianity immediately adopted the codex as its privileged form . . . Christians and Jews actively differentiated themselves from each other through the adoption of the book or the scroll. The crucial thing for Christians was to make sure that they read *their* Jewish scriptures in a form that was materially as unlike the Jewish scriptures as possible.[19]

As Christianity overtook Europe, so, too, did the codex. As Marshall McLuhan observed, "the medium is the message." At this point in the history of the book, a codex would signal a Christian text; a roll, on the other hand, would signal a Jewish text. For example, let's return to the eighth-century Book of Esther roll from Chapter One. The eighth century might seem at first a late date for a roll. However, considering that the Book of Esther is an important text in the Hebrew Bible (as well as the Christian Old Testament), it is appropriate that it appeared as a roll. Indeed, we might infer from its format that this particular roll's first audience was Jewish, not Christian.

Finally, perhaps the principal reason why the codex ended up as the main writing medium was functionality. The codex allowed random access to the information it contained. As with its forbearer, the wax tablet, a reader using a codex book could open to any part of the text in an instant. While wax tablets might have three of four leaves made of wood, the codex might have hundreds of leaves of papyrus or parchment, and later paper—leaves that were immediately accessible to the reader. This was made possible by the way in which the leaves were gathered and bound together, which will be examined later in this chapter. The roll or scroll, on the other hand, allowed for linear access to text written only on the recto side of the roll. Due to the nature of this format, a reader had to scroll forward or backward to arrive at specific sections of a text.

In the history of communication media, formats offering random access to information generally tend to triumph over formats offering linear access. In recent history, this can be seen in the example of the audio cassette tape. If a listener had just listened to a song on a cassette and wanted to play it again, he or she was required to rewind the tape to that point. This is linear access. The same concept applies to a movie on a VHS cassette. Contrast these examples with a CD or a digital music file, or a DVD or digital file of a movie. These formats offer random access (and arguably superior sound and image quality), which made these formats more desirable.

Codex Sinaiticus

For the first few centuries of the Common Era, Greek and Latin texts found in codices were usually written on papyrus. In this way, papyrus rolls evolved into papyrus codices. Eventually, papyrus codices gave way to parchment codices. As we have seen, papyrus as a substrate for writing has a number of drawbacks. For example, papyrus is a natural resource found primarily in Egypt, and therefore it had to be imported into other regions. Parchment as a material used in books, on the other hand, is much more durable, flexible, and is made from a natural resource that can be cultivated almost anywhere in the world.

One of the most dramatic early uses of parchment in a codex survives from the mid-fourth century in the form of the *Codex Sinaiticus*. This manuscript takes its name from Mount Sinai, because most of the book was discovered in the mid-19th century at St. Catherine's monastery on Mount Sinai. The book is now preserved at the British Library, with other remaining portions scattered across other libraries. The religious significance of the *Codex Sinaiticus* is immense—it contains the oldest complete manuscript of the New Testament.[20] Its significance in the history of the book is also immense, especially considering its physical form. Its four columns of text per page bring to mind how text might be laid out on a roll from that period, but instead of one continuous sheet rolled up, we have the page divisions of a codex book. Instead of papyrus, the manuscript makes use of parchment. All in all, the *Codex Sinaiticus* is a hybrid that speaks to the book in an exciting state of evolution. To view the *Codex Sinaiticus* and learn more about its history, please visit the British Library's https://www.bl.uk/collection-items/codex-sinaiticus.

Manuscripts in Medieval Europe

The evolution of the book into the form in which we know it today took place through the Middle Ages and early modern periods in Europe. The Middle Ages, also known as the medieval period in Europe, date from roughly the fifth century CE to the early 15th century—that is, the fall of the Roman Empire through the onset of the European Renaissance. During the European Middle Ages, the major form of the book was the manuscript codex. The technology of printing in Europe did not emerge until the mid-15th century; thus books produced in the Middle Ages were all written out by hand by scribes. Today these books are commonly referred to as medieval manuscripts. "Manu" in Latin means "hand"; "scriptus" from "scribo" means "to write."

Parchment

The primary natural resource used for producing medieval manuscripts was the skin of domestic animals. The *pages* of a manuscript book were produced from animal skins that had been stretched and scraped. The covering material used for *binding* a manuscript book were often made of leather—that is, animal skins that had been tanned and made more durable.

Parchment is a general term for the skin of an animal that has been prepared to be used as a writing surface. Typically, the animal used was a sheep, calf, or goat. "Vellum" is also a term for animal skin used for this purpose but, technically, its meaning is more specific. The word originates from the Old French "velin" meaning "calf" and thus refers to calfskin.[21] Vellum has also been used as a term for the skin of other young domestic animals (lambs or kids), and in more recent years it has been used as a broader term for animal skin. In this way, "parchment" and "vellum" have become interchangeable. For example, in the antiquarian book world, you might often hear a parchment bookbinding referred to as a vellum binding (as a general term and not necessarily meaning a calfskin binding). The type of animal skin used to create parchment is usually not immediately identifiable. Once the skin of an animal has been prepared as a writing surface, it is not obvious what animal it once was—as opposed to leather prepared as binding material, where a close look usually reveals the animal from which it was produced.

Parchment as a natural resource is plentiful in any geographic region where livestock is raised. This means, of course, that parchment is accessible in most parts of the world. The process of making parchment is unpleasant to say the least and, judging from the reactions of some of my students, "totally gross" (and they are spared the smells!). First it must be recognized that skin has two sides: the hair side and flesh side. The hair side, or grain side, is the side that is visible on a living animal—the side out of which hair grows. It is the side that faces outward, so it might have discoloration, damage, or scars. Pause from reading and look down at your hand or arm, and you will see the hair side of your own skin. The flesh side is the side you cannot see. It faces inward into the body, and is, to some degree, protected by the outer layers of the skin. When looking at a medieval manuscript, the hair and flesh sides are often easily identifiable. The hair side has hair follicles and is usually darker and rougher than the flesh side, which is typically smoother and lighter in color.

The first step in making parchment from animal skin is to soak the skin of a sheep, goat, or calf in a solution of lime and water for about a week. This loosens the hair from the hair side and the fat and other biological gunk attached to the flesh side. The skin is then draped over a beam—but not yet stretched. Both sides are scraped to further remove any unwanted material from the skin. It is then washed in water, dried, and stretched on a frame.[22] As skin dries, it naturally shrinks. Stretching the skin on a frame prevents this from happening and keeps the skin's surface as large as possible.

Figure 2-3 shows an image of a stretched animal skin being scraped. In this image, we can see a parchment maker using a crescent-shaped knife, appropriately called a lunellum. The shape of the lunellum and its lack of

Figure 2-3 "The parchment maker." Reproduction of an engraving by Christoph Weigel, 1698. The New York Times Museum of the Recorded Word. RIT Cary Graphic Arts Collection. Photograph by Jiageng Lin.

pointed corners helps to prevent the animal skin from being punctured during the scraping process. As the skin is scraped, any remaining hair and fat is removed, creating a thin, cleaner parchment. The more that the skin was scraped away, the finer the parchment. Historians once thought, for example, that the finest parchment was uterine vellum, that is, skin taken from an aborted calf. This very fine, thin skin feels almost like tissue paper. Recent scholarship, however, sheds doubt on this notion, noting that the quantity of uterine vellum needed to produce books seems to be unrealistic. Instead, scholars think what was thought to be uterine calf might just be skin scraped with great skill until it is light and airy. Or, perhaps, the skin was carefully split into two halves, a technique that also can be done with early paper.[23] The takeaway here is that there were different qualities of parchment, just as there are different qualities of paper and other writing surfaces.

As earlier examples in this book have shown, natural resources shape our technology and how we use it. That is absolutely the case with parchment, which literally gives shape to our writing surfaces. When the skin of a livestock animal (sans legs) is stretched, its shape is naturally rectangular, reflecting the body shapes of the animals. Thus, the natural shape of animals results in the rectangular shape of books, which had already been established to some degree with clay, wax tablets, and rolls.

Making a Medieval Manuscript

Once a parchment skin is scraped, stretched, and dried. it is trimmed to a more defined rectangular shape. The result is one sheet of parchment. Figure 2-4 shows a large leaf held at the Cary Collection from a 16th-century antiphonal or choir book. Measuring 34 inches tall by 23.75 inches wide (86.36×60.325 cm), it likely constitutes the trimmed skin of one animal. Both sides of this sheet were used for text, thus generating one leaf or two pages. To create more writing surfaces

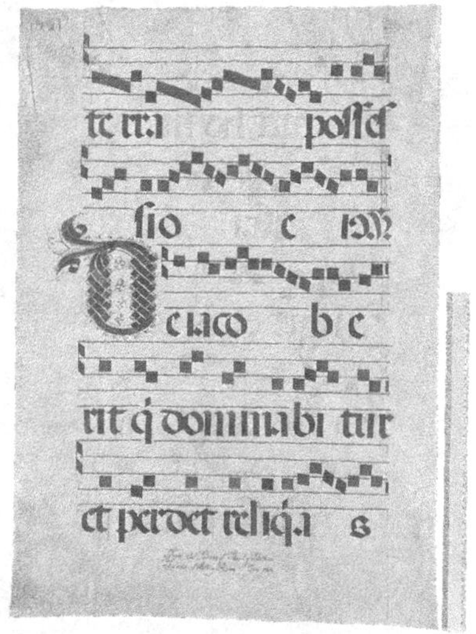

Figure 2-4   A leaf from a choir book, Spain, 16th century. RIT Cary Graphic Arts Collection.

(more pages) from out of one parchment sheet, the sheet could be folded. When a parchment sheet is folded once, for example, it creates a bifolium, that is, a folded sheet consisting of two leaves or four pages. In book terminology, each individual unit of parchment (and later paper) in a book is a leaf. Each leaf has two sides or pages. The front, or right-hand side of the leaf is called the recto. The back side is the verso.

Figure 2-5 from the Cary Collection is a bifolium that once resided within a late 15th-century music manuscript book from Venice. It measures 19.375 inches tall by 27.875 wide (49.2 × 70.8 cm). All four pages have been written on. A blank bifolium of parchment was where most manuscript book production began. The next steps in the process were the work of a scribe.

Figure 2-5 A bifolium from a music manuscript, Venice, Italy, 15th century. RIT Cary Graphic Arts Collection. Photograph by Elizabeth Lamark.

Scribes

Who were medieval scribes, and how did they create medieval books? As Christopher De Hamel notes, prior to about 1110 CE, scribes were monks working in a scriptorium, a room in a monastery dedicated to writing. From about 1200 onward, scribes were professional, secular laborers. As De Hamel writes, "By 1300 it must have been exceptional for a monastery to make its own manuscripts: usually, monks bought their books from shops like everyone else."[24]

The scribe's first step in preparing parchment for writing was ruling each page. As we saw in our earlier discussions of cuneiform tablets and papyrus, the practice of writing on a lined surface dates to ancient times and continues today. Just as most modern writers prefer a ruled surface, so, too, did medieval scribes. To get lines spaced evenly on the sheet, the scribe first pricked each sheet along its long edges with evenly spaced

Figure 2-6 Pricking and ruling on a Bible leaf, England, 13th century. RIT Cary Graphic Arts Collection. Photograph by Elizabeth Lamark.

holes. To do this, the scribe used the tip of a knife or a "star wheel," which might be best described as a spur or spiked wheel attached to a handle that could be rolled over the parchment, piercing evenly spaced holes in the parchment. The scribe often pricked many parchment sheets at once.

After the scribe had pricked the parchment, he ruled the pages. Using a lead ruler, the scribe drew lines from each perforation on one side of the page to the corresponding perforation on the other side. Up until about 1100 CE, a scribe might not draw visible lines, but would instead score the parchment with a stylus in dry point. From about that time through the 13th century, scribes typically ruled pages using a lead pencil called a plummet. Thereafter, scribes would often rule the page in ink.[25] Figure 2-6 is a detail of a leaf from an early 13th-century English Bible held at the Cary Collection. Not only are the perforations clearly visible, but so too is the ink ruling derived from them. In addition to ruling the page, the scribe would also lay out the page with faint lines designating spaces for text, decorative initial letters, illustrations, and margins.

As depicted in Figure 2-7, scribes worked at sloped desks. The texts they wrote were typically copied from existing manuscripts; therefore, scribes often had an exemplar text on their desks beside their blank parchment. Some medieval illustrations depict scribes writing at sophisticated desks that have a second lectern hovering over the desk, holding the exemplar at about eye level. Sometimes scribes wrote out original texts. In this case, they copied texts prepared on "wax tablets or scrap parchment."[26]

Scribes worked holding tools in each hand. In one hand, usually the right, they held quill pens made from a feather of large bird.[27] As De Hamel writes, "The best feathers prove to be the five or so outer wing pinions of goose or swan."[28] Quill pens were produced by fashioning a nib at the tip of the feather by cutting the tip at a steep angle and adding a small slit.[29] Typically, all the barbs of the feather were removed to make the quill easier to hold. Thus, in medieval illustrations of scribes, the quill does not often look like a feather, but rather like they are holding pens or long bones. This is just the rachis or shaft of the feather.

The quill was cut with a penknife, which is what scribes typically held in their other hand. When not using it for cutting the quill, a scribe would use a penknife to hold the parchment steady and to erase or scrape away any mistakes. My first medieval studies teacher compared the way scribes held their quill and penknife to the way Europeans hold their cutlery while eating—an apt description.[30]

Figure 2-7 A medieval scribe. Reproduced from a manuscript miniature, Bruges, Beligum, c. 1456. The New York Times Museum of the Recorded Word. RIT Cary Graphic Arts Collection. Photograph by Jiageng Lin.

Fitted into a hole in the surface of a scribe's desk would be an inkhorn, that is, the horn of an animal that had been hollowed out so that it could hold the liquid ink. A quill held a fair amount of ink, but the scribe would often return to the inkhorn. Black ink was used primarily for text. Through the Middles Ages, black ink was made in two ways. First, ink might be fashioned in a manner similar to the ink used in ancient Egypt—a mixture of carbon (often lampblack) mixed with gum arabic, which served as a binder. It also might be made from a mixture of crushed up oak gall, ground iron sulfate, and gum arabic.[31] Oak galls are small, round plant growths produced when wasps lay eggs in oak bark. The insides of oak galls are rich in tannins, which serve to create the black pigment.

Inks came in other colors too. In addition to black, red and blue inks made from natural pigments were often used. Red ink might be derived from vermillion or burnt sienna, blue from ultramarine or lapis lazuli. Other colors include green from verdigris, yellow from saffron, and white from white lead. Such natural pigments provided a variety of hues with which to beautify manuscripts. Figure 2-8 is an instructive example of the

Figure 2-8   A leaf from a Bible, Germany, 15th century. RIT Cary Graphic Arts Collection.

use of color in a German 15th-century Bible. Here, as was often the case, color helps guide the reader through the layout of the text. The large blue "H" begins Ezra 8, as does the text written in red "Cap. viii," short for the Latin "capitulus," or "chapter." A stroke of red ink also highlights the capital letter at that beginning of each sentence. You might also note the hole in the parchment. Sometimes, in the process of stretching, parchment might tear, resulting in a hole. If that were to happen, the parchment, which came at some expense, was still used. The scribe simply wrote around the hole. Alternatively, the hole might be sewn up, just like human skin receiving stitches.

Illuminated Manuscripts

"Illuminated" is the term used to describe manuscripts that have been decorated with vibrant colors and/or the application of gold or silver leaf. These embellishments might take the form of ornate borders or decorative initial letters. If a decorated initial letter portrays people or a scene, it is referred to as an historiated initial. As with the example of the German Bible above, decoration is often functional. Figure 2-9 provides an example from a 14th-century Italian Bible leaf from the Cary Collection. In a manner similar to the use of a drop cap in modern typography, a large splendid "P" brings the reader's eye right to the beginning of a new passage. Once again, illumination is not only elegant decoration, but also a guide to help the reader navigate the page. As a test, look at a page of a medieval manuscript, whether in person or using a color image. As a modern reader, you might not understand the language (usually Latin), and you might readily read the blackletter handwriting, but notice how the page layout and decorative elements guide your eyes in a familiar way.

Illumination, in a more precise definition of the word, is the art of adding gold or silver to the page and burnishing it so that light causes it to shine or illuminate. Gold illumination is most common. The process of applying gold illumination begins with preparing gold leaf. Gold, which is very malleable, is pounded and flattened until it is very, very thin—"Like gold to airy thinness beat," as the poet John Donne describes it in "A Valediction: Forbidding Mourning."[32] Gold can be applied to the page in several ways. Most commonly, gold leaf is affixed using an adhesive made of egg white and water. Gold might also be laid on a foundation of gesso (plaster of Paris) that has been applied to the page. This gives the gold leaf a more three-dimensional appearance. Finally, gold could be

Figure 2-9 A leaf from a Bible, Italy, 14th century. RIT Cary Graphic Arts Collection.

added to the page by crafting a gold ink by mixing powdered gold and a binding agent such as gum arabic. Gold is usually applied to the page before any other decoration, so that when it is burnished, none of the other colored ink or paint is smeared.

The artisan responsible for applying decoration to the page is called an illuminator. In the workflow of the production of a medieval manuscript, the scribe and the illuminator were usually two different people who performed two different jobs. The scribe's main responsibility was writing out the text—what you see primarily in black on a medieval manuscript. As the scribe wrote out the text, space was left intentionally for the addition of decorative elements such as illuminated initials. These elements were added by the illuminator. This was the usual division of labor. Once the scribe's work was finished, the sheets were then handed over to the illuminator for the decoration. Although the scribe may have left space for illumination, that does not necessarily mean that the space was always filled. Figure 2-10, for example, shows a 16th-century manuscript of Boccaccio's *Decameron*. Here the scribe has left space for an initial "G" that was never added by an illuminator. Someone penciled in the letter, however, likely at much later date.

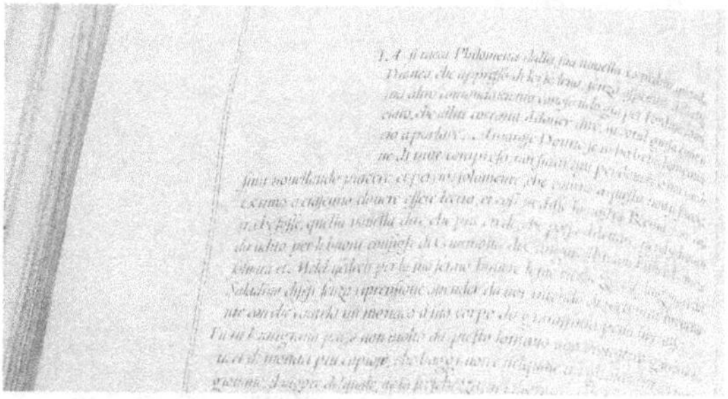

Figure 2-10 Giovanni Boccaccio, *The Decameron*, manuscript (S.l., c. 16th century). RIT Cary Graphic Arts Collection. Photograph by Elizabeth Lamark.

Gold leaf could also be applied to the edges of books, producing gilt edges. This method of beautifying books dates to the 15th century and became a common feature of books that endures to the present.[33] As with the application of gold leaf to pages, gold leaf may be applied to the edges of books with adhesive made from egg white and water. Each edge of the book (head, tail, fore-edge) may have gold leaf applied, although sometimes gold might be applied only to the head, or perhaps just the head and fore-edge; this is because these edges are most exposed (the tail edge typically rested on a shelf, particularly from the 17th century onward). The head and fore-edges are exposed to dust, moisture, and other potential harmful elements. A gilt edge helps to protect the parchment or paper. In this way, the gold is not just decorative; it also creates a protective layer.

Blackletter

The style of handwriting used throughout most of the European Middle Ages is generally referred to as blackletter, though gothic might also be used. Blackletter is a broad category within which exists various handwriting forms from roughly 900 CE to 1500 CE. The blackletter style of writing is characterized by short downward strokes—movements that naturally were suited to the nib of a quill, as opposed to the more rounded letterforms such as Roman inscription or the earlier Carolingian handwriting in the eighth and ninth centuries CE.[34] These earlier forms were seen again in the early 15th century as humanists revived ancient texts and the Carolingian handwriting that they believed to be more legible.[35] Blackletter's influence on letterforms is another example of humans adapting to writing technology. The design of the letterforms evolved because of the nature of the nib of the quill.

How Long Did Manuscripts Take to Make?

Writing out books by hand took time, the length of which depended on the length of the text and the skills of the scribes. It also depended on who the scribe was, and what other responsibilities he might have. If the scribe was a monk, as was usually the case in the early Middle Ages, then producing manuscripts was likely not his only responsibility. Writing might be just one part of day filled with prayer, food preparation, herding, etc. Clemens estimates that for monastic scribes "a good rate of production for such a scribe would probably have been between 150–200 lines of text a day."[36] With this in mind, according to De Hamel, a scribe working in a monastery might "achieve three or four moderate-sized books a year."[37] Professional scribes worked at a much quicker and dedicated pace, producing a *Book of Hours,* a relatively short book, in a week.[38] A text of a moderate length could take a month. A longer, decorative manuscript might take over a year.[39]

Incipits and Explicits

Like earlier book technologies, medieval manuscripts often provided bibliographic information that identified the title and author of the text, when and where it was written, and sometimes even the identity of the scribe who performed the work. Medieval manuscripts, like their tablet and roll predecessors, usually supplied this information at the end of the text in a colophon. As defined in Chapter One, a colophon is the "finishing stroke," a concluding passage that provides information about the book. A similar term for this section of the manuscript book is the "explicit," Latin for "here ends." Considering the tremendous amount of time and labor it could take to complete a manuscript book, it is no wonder that, when some monks ended their work, they wrote out explicits that not only identified the texts and when they were finished, but also thanked God for their having completed their tasks. Scribes might also express their weariness. Several very humorous explicits survive, for example:

"Explicit hic totum pro Christi da mihi potum!"
"Now I've written the whole thing; for Christ's sake give me a drink!"[40]

If medieval manuscript books had endings in the form of an explicit, then it is only natural that they should begin with an "incipit," Latin for

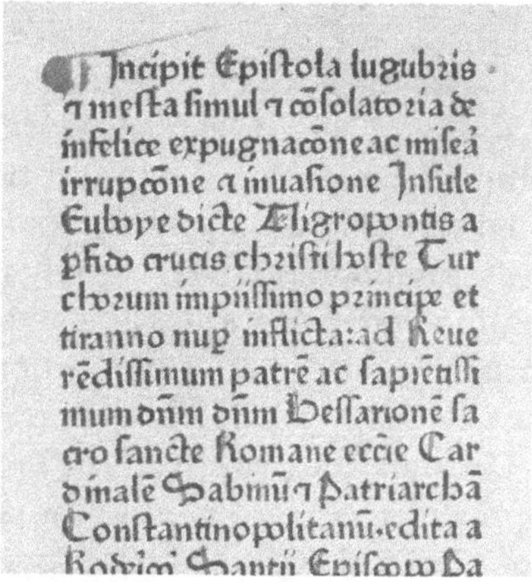

> ⁋ Incipit Epiſtola lugubꝛis · ꞇ meſta ſimul ꞇ cõſolatoꝛia ⸄ infelice expugnacõne ac miſeä irrupcõne a inuaſione Jnſule Euⸯⸯpe ⸄icte Æligroⱬⱬntis a ⱬⱬⱬⱬ crucis chꝛiſtilⱬſte Cur clⱬꝛum impiíſſimo pꝛincipe et tíranno nuⱬ inflicta꞉ad Reue rediſſimum patrē ac ſapícuſſi mumõm õm Beſſarionē ſa cꞏo ſancte Romane eccie Car õmale Sⱬabmü ꞇ Patriarchã Conſtantinopolitanü·edíta a Roſuící Sⱬantíí Epiſcⱬⱬ Da

Figure 2-11   Rodericus Zamorensis, *Epistola de expugnatione Nigropontis* (Cologne: Ulrich Zel, c. 1470–1471). RIT Cary Graphic Arts Collection. Photograph by Jordan Funk.

"here begins." In this way, the first page of text might begin with the word "Incipit" followed by the title or general description of the text. This was usually how these early books began. Medieval manuscript books rarely had title pages. Title pages did not become a common feature of books until decades after Johannes Gutenberg invented his method of printing in the 1450s.[41] Other preliminary matter that is now found at the beginning of books, such as half-title pages or tables of contents, would also later become standard features in books. The texts of books simply began.

Incipits and explicits are also found in the earliest *printed* books. For example, figure 2-11 shows the incipit from a pamphlet printed in c. 1470 reporting on the Turkish siege of Negroponte (Euboea) from the Venetian Empire. This report is one of the first instances of contemporary news being printed. The text begins:

> "Incipit Epistola lugubris et mesta simul et consolatoria de infelice expugnacione ac misera irrupcione et inuasione Insule Euboye dicte Nigropontis."
>
> *"Here begins a sad and mournful, and at the same time, consolatory letter on the unfortunate invasion and sad intrusion and assault of the Island Euboea called Negroponte."*[42]

Gathering the Leaves

When the scribe and illuminator had finished their work, the sheets were ready to be assembled into a book. Finished sheets were gathered together into quires, also sometimes called gatherings, particularly when describing a printed book. A quire is a set of folded sheets, perhaps two, four, or six, that are nested together. Typically, in a medieval manuscript, the sheets were arranged so that flesh side faced flesh side, and hair side faced hair side.[43] This arrangement often creates a striking visual effect, as each opening offers a brighter or darker contrast than the last.

In order to ensure that the sheets were gathered in the proper sequence, scribes often wrote a "catchword" at the bottom of the last page of each quire. This catchword matches the first word that appears at the beginning of the first line of text of the subsequent quire. In this way, when stacking the quires, the bookbinder could match the catchword of each quire to the corresponding word beginning the next quire, thus keeping the quires in the correct order.[44] Scribes would also use signatures to help organize the quires. In this system, each quire was designated with a letter, and each leaf a number. So, for example, in a quire of two sheets, a scribe might write "a1" in the lower corner of the recto (right-hand side) of the first leaf, "a2" on the recto of the second leaf.[45] The subsequent "a3" and "a4" on the final two leaves in the quire would likely not be written, as they are implied. The next quires would run "b1, b2" and "c1, c2" and so forth. The use of catchwords and signatures have roots in the organizing systems of cuneiform tablets, and would continue in printed books.

Bookbinding

Once the quires had been assembled in the correct order, they were ready to be bound. Generally, the anatomy of a bound book from the European Middle Ages and Renaissance consisted of three major parts: the text block, the boards, and the covering material. The text block was the stack of assembled quires. This was the content of the book and was therefore the most vital part of the book. Sometimes books from the medieval and Renaissance periods in Europe consisted only of a sewn text block, which could be used by readers without ever being bound.

When a book was to be bound, the quires of the text block were sewn together using sewing supports. Sewing supports were strips made of material such as cord or alum-tawed skin that ran perpendicular to the text block. Picture the spine of an early book resting vertically on a shelf. There might be several horizontal ridges on the spine. These bands are the raised sewing supports found underneath the binding material. Figure 2-12 shows quires of a book in a sewing frame with sewing supports running at right angle to the quires. The bookbinder would sew each quire to the sewing supports by running thread through corresponding holes in the center (or gutter) of each quire and around each sewing support. After traveling

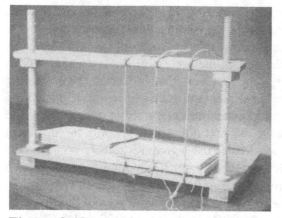

Figure 2-12   Quires on a sewing frame. Florence O. Bean and John C. Brodhead, *Bookbinding for Beginners* (Boston, Mass.: School Arts Pub. Co., 1914), Plate LI, p. 77.

the length of the quire, the last stich was made up to the next quire. Then that quire would be attached to each sewing support in the same manner. In this way, the bookbinder would attach each quire one at a time until the stack of quires was secured to the sewing supports and to each other. The use of sewing supports appears to have been invented in Europe beginning around the eighth century.[46] Earlier bindings in both the Middle East and Europe did not yet use sewing supports, but rather had quires that were link-stitched together. In this binding style, the quires were sewn together with linking, vertical stitches at several places along the spine.

Figure 2-13 is a late 14th-century manuscript book preserved at the Cary Collection. At some point in its life, its binding covering was removed, perhaps to prepare it for rebinding. For some reason, the book

Figure 2-13   *Statuta antiqua et nova ordinis Cartusiensis*, Manuscript (Germany?, c. 1370–1390). RIT Cary Graphic Arts Collection. Photograph by Elizabeth Lamark.

never was rebound, but this has served useful to students and scholars who wish to study the anatomy of medieval books. Examining the spine of the book, you can see how the individual quires are gathered, stacked, and sewn together onto sewing supports.

The cords of the sewing support had a second important purpose. They would attach to the second major part of the bound book—the boards. The front and back boards, or covers, served to protect the text block. During the medieval period, the boards of a book were often made of hardwood such as oak and beech (the former being used primarily in England and northern Europe, the latter being used in the southern Europe). Wooden boards are an inheritance of the structure of wax tablets, which were still being used through the medieval period. Two boards were cut to a size that fit the text block. Channels corresponding to the locations of the sewing supports were cut into the edges of the boards. Excess cord from the sewing supports was run through the channels, attaching the boards to the text block. In addition to wood, the front and back boards could also be made from pasteboard. Akin to our modern cardboard, pasteboard was created by pasting layers of parchment or paper together.[47]

Figure 2-14 shows a binding structure with wooden boards from a *printed* book from 1743. It is a copy of the Bible printed in 1743 by Christoph Sauer in Germantown, Pennsylvania. Known colloquially as the Sauer Bible, this printing of Luther's German translation was the second edition of the Bible ever printed in the United States. This copy appears to have been prepared for rebinding that was never completed. The lack of binding material affords the opportunity to examine the book's anatomy. Although well out of the medieval period, the binding reflects a similar general structure. The quires or gatherings have been stacked together into a text block that has been sewn onto five sewing supports, each consisting of two cords. The cords are attached to front and back wooden boards. Nearly all the covering material has been removed, with only remnants of leather remaining on one corner of the boards. The covering material that once wrapped around the boards and spine of the book is the final part of a bound book.

During the European Middle Ages, books were covered with animal skin, usually leather, though parchment was

Figure 2-14 *Biblia, das ist: die Heilige Schrift Altes und Neue* (Germantown, Pa.: Gedruckt bey Chistoph Saur, 1743). RIT Cary Graphic Arts Collection.

also used. Commonly used skins include calf, goat, and pig. The leather was wrapped around the spine and boards, with tabs or "turn-ins" folded over the edges of the boards and pasted onto their insides.

Some bindings did not use boards of wood or pasteboard, but simply consisted of a covering material that was fairly rigid. A limp parchment binding is an example of such a style. In this case, parchment was attached directly to a text block using the cords from the sewing supports. A variation on this theme is a semi-limp parchment binding, in which the parchment covering was strengthened by the addition of a sheet of paper or parchment.

A helpful feature found on surviving bindings from the medieval period (and often shown in contemporary depictions of books) are clasps. Book clasps were often attached in pairs to the front and back boards, and fastened together to hold the book securely. This is especially helpful when the leaves are made from parchment. Parchment is hygroscopic and therefore is absorbing water depending on its surrounding environmental conditions. When parchment leaves in a book are too dry, they shrink and pull back; when they take on water, they expand. Clasps hold the boards together tight, which helps to stabilize the parchment text block. Paper is also hygroscopic, but less dramatically so. Clasps on bindings with text blocks made of paper, whether manuscript or print, are less functional, but they had become a popular feature on books and so they continued to be used. Indeed, clasps may still be found on some 21st-century books.[48]

Girdle Books

One of the more interesting forms bookbinding took in the later Middle Ages speaks to the portable nature of books. Appearing as far back as the late 13th century, girdle books employed a functional bookbinding style associated with monks and others who carried holy texts with them.[49] Girdle books were wrapped in leather, which extended out from the tail edges of the book into a large knot that could be wrapped around and hung from a belt. Thus, a monk or another reader who benefitted from having a portable book could travel with a book hanging from his belt. Figure 2-15 is a model of a girdle binding made by well-known bookbinder and educator J. Franklin Mowery. Perhaps such a style could make a comeback in modern times. Can you imagine commuters on trains reading paperbacks or even Kindles that hang from their belts?

Size

Generally speaking, the size of books tells us about how they might have been read and what sort of texts they might contain. Take, for example, the large 16th-century choir book leaf shown in figure 2-4. If asked how this manuscript was likely used, the size of the leaf might immediately suggest that it was read and performed by a group of singers. Indeed, this text was clearly meant to be large enough to be viewed by many people at once.

Considering notions of size, many of the forms of the book that predate the Middle Ages are handhelds—clay and wax tablets, papyrus rolls. Manuscript books in the Middle Ages could be quite weighty. Theological works, for example, could be heavy tomes more suited for reading at a lectern than casually at a table. So far, in this brief history of the book, reading and writing media have started off relatively small and remained more of a handheld size. Moving forward in history, there becomes a more general reoccurring trend in which reading and writing technologies evolve from larger objects to handheld objects. This is generally true for medieval manuscripts, where the overall trend is a move from larger books to smaller books. Scholars have documented how Bibles and other theological works

Figure 2-15 A modern reproduction of a medieval girdle binding made by J. Franklin Mowery. RIT Cary Graphic Arts Collection.

that were quite large in the 11th and 12th centuries were reduced in size in the 13th and 14th centuries. For example, see Christopher De Hamel, *The Book. A History of the Bible* (London; New York: Phaidon, 2001),

114–117. *Books of Hours*, for example, were personal prayer books. Readers could carry them while they traveled, and they could be comfortably read anywhere that there was adequate light. Such books were generally about the size of a modern paperback, or even a modern e-book reader. This is the size of a reading device with which humans appear to be most comfortable—something that can be held in one's hand at a comfortable reading distance from the eye to the text.

Reuse

Ancient technologies were often reusable. Clay and wax tablets could be written on, erased, and then written on again. The recto side of a papyrus roll could be erased and reused, or, if space were needed, a scribe might write on the previously unused verso side of the roll. Medieval manuscripts continued the trend of readable/writable functions in books. What's more, they were also recyclable.

Earlier we saw how a scribe held both a quill with which to write, and a penknife with which to erase or scrape away ink. In this way, parchment manuscripts are erasable while being written. When the ink dries, it is not as easy to erase, but it can be done. Parchment is a tough material that can sustain some amount of scraping for minor erasure. Sometimes manuscript books were completely erased and their newly blank leaves reused for a new text or texts. Such a manuscript is called a palimpsest. Erasing and reusing an existing book so that a different text could be written out is a method of producing a book without the expense of acquiring new parchment on which to write. Books chosen to be palimpsested might be texts that book owners no longer found useful.

Creating a palimpsest began by disbinding a book (the opposite process of gathering and sewing up quires). The loose parchment bifolia were then washed with a mixture using an acidic liquid such

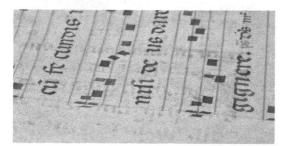

Figure 2-16   Detail of a leaf from a palimpsest. The overtext is an Italian antiphonal, c. 1460. The undertext is a gradual, c. 1300. RIT Cary Graphic Arts Collection.

as orange juice or milk in order to erase the ink.[50] The leaves were dried and polished with a pumice stone to remove any remaining ink. At the end of this process, very little, if any, of the original text is visible. Typically, the bifolia were then cut in half and rotated 90 degrees, creating a new stack of blank leaves ready to be written upon. Figure 2-16, for example, shows a detail of leaf from an Italian antiphonal (c. 1460) from the Cary Collection. The antiphonal text was written over an erased gradual (c. 1300). In this case, a fair amount of the erased undertext is still visible running perpendicular to the new text.

Recently, more scholars are studying surviving palimpsests, trying to recover the undertexts that have been erased. This can be done using spectral imaging to collect and process images of palimpsests, using different bands of light. If successful, different spectral conditions can cause the once-erased pigments to react and reveal themselves. This can result in the recovery of important texts that had been thought lost. Sometimes the discovery can be quite dramatic. Perhaps the most famous example is the Archimedes Palimpsest. This 13th-century prayer book was written on palimpsested pages that contain two tracts of Archimedes written out in the 10th century. These tracts, *Stomachion* and *The Method of Mechanical Theorems*, were once thought lost to history.[51] From about 2000 to the present, scholars have been imaging this palimpsest, allowing these works of Archimedes to be read for the first time in a millennium.

Recycling medieval manuscripts could also mean reusing the parchment in other creative ways. As a resource, parchment was durable; therefore, it was not something to be thrown away. One of the most common uses for undesired manuscript leaves was to be reused as material for later *printed* books. Sometimes it reused for what is called "binder's waste." Figure 2-17,

Figure 2-17 Manuscript used as binding waste in Origen, *Operū Origenis Adamātii tomi duo priores* (Paris: In edibus J. parvi et J. Badii Ascensii, 1519–1522). RIT Cary Graphic Arts Collection.

for example, is an edition of the works of Origen of Alexandria (c. 184–c. 253) printed in Paris in 1519–1522 and now held at the Cary Collection.[52] Visible in the book's gutter between the inside front cover and the title page is a manuscript fragment that is wrapped around the spine to the inside back cover. This piece of parchment is a spine lining that reinforces the spine and attaches to the boards. If you look carefully, you can see the prick marks and ruling that were made by an earlier scribe. Occasionally, interesting texts are found hidden in binder's waste. For example, while conserving the binding of a volume of medical texts from 1578 held at the Folger Shakespeare Library, conservator J. Franklin Mowery uncovered a fragment of a copy of Eusebins's fourth-century work *Historia ecclesiastica* that dated to the seventh century. This fragment happens possibly to be "the earliest surviving manuscript written in England."[53] More discoveries such as this one surely are to be made.

More dramatically, manuscript leaves are sometimes used as bookbinding material for other books. Figure 2-18 shows a biography of Saint Francisco de Borja from 1613, bound in a leaf from an earlier Latin manuscript of the *Lives of the Saints*.[54] Using a recycled manuscript in a bookbinding is an economical way of covering a book. Parchment bindings, as opposed to those with leather coverings, were already a less expensive option. Using recycled material helped lower the price further still, while also providing a durable binding material.

Figure 2-18 Manuscript as a bookbinding for Pedro de Ribadeneyra, *Leben Francisci Borgiae: dritten Generals der Societet Iesu* (Getruckt zu Ingolstatt: Durch Andream Angermayr, 1613). RIT Cary Graphic Arts Collection. Photograph by Elizabeth Lamark.

Book Storage

What was the price of these books and who was reading them? The most expensive part of making manuscript books was the parchment. Books,

MODERN ADS FOR EARLY TECHNOLOGIES

Medieval Manuscript. Designed by Amelia Fontanel.

The Medieval Manuscript Book

Memory: The codex form has the ability to hold a great deal of text in one volume. If a book has a very large number of leaves, the volume may get too unwieldy, to the point where it is difficult to bind. At this point, the text can carry over into additional bound volumes.

Readable/writable: Parchment was the primary material used for making manuscript books in the medieval period. Parchment is a very durable substrate, and writing can be erased by scraping the ink off with a pen knife. Parchment that has been used for a manuscript book can also be completely erased and reused, a process called palimpsesting.

Recyclable: The durability of parchment made it a vital resource that could be reused in a variety of ways rather than being thrown away. These include bibliographic reuses such as bookbinding.

Durability: Parchment is very durable, so the text blocks of medieval manuscript books can last thousands of years, as surviving early parchment has demonstrated. The bindings on manuscript books are less durable, especially if the book is heavily used. While contemporary bookbindings have survived, in general they need to be repaired or replaced over time as needed.

Security: Similar to the wax tablets that influenced the codex, manuscript books were usually protected by bookbindings that often included wooden boards. There were many binding options, ranging from simple limp parchment to heavy leather over wood or pasteboard. Endpapers between the binding and the title page also help protect the body of text.

Access: One of the factors that distinguished the codex from the roll or scroll is its ability to offer random access to its users. That is, a reader can access any part of the text at any time, without the need for scrolling forward or backward.

Cost: $$–$$$$. The cost of a manuscript book often depended on the length of the text. Typically, the longer the text, the larger the amount of parchment was needed. Preparing a manuscript book from newly acquired parchment would be more expensive then palimpsesting and reusing an existing parchment book. If the book buyer wanted his or her book decorated by an illuminator, then this would add further cost. Finally, the choice of a binding could run from something simple to something rather elaborate.

therefore, were priced by the quire or gathering, and could get quite expensive. Needless to say, books were not commonly owned in the Middle Ages, and literacy rates were low. Scott D. N. Cook cautiously estimates illiteracy rates in "fifteenth-century Europe at well over 90 percent of the general population."[55] If individuals owned manuscript books, they probably did not own many. They could store their books in small chests or in cupboards, like other household items.[56] As the production of books grew, so too did book ownership, particular in monasteries, cathedrals, and universities. This led to advances in storage methods and an increase in the sizes of spaces that held books. As Elmer D. Johnson describes:

> Toward the end of the Middle Ages, in the 14th and 15th centuries, there were many physical changes in the monastic and cathedral libraries. The number of books increased, in most cases from a few hundred to a few thousand. The armaria, or book-chests, had given way to book closets and then to small library rooms. By the 15th century, some religious institutions were constructing separate library buildings.[57]

Later in the medieval period, books begin to migrate to shelves. In monasteries, universities, or wherever books might be made available to multiple readers, books would sometimes be chained to desks or shelves to ensure that none would go missing. This is the concept of the chained library. The most sensible place to attach a chain to a book was on the upper or mid fore-edge of one of the boards. The book was then placed on the shelf with its spine in and its fore-edge facing out, so that the chain rested in front of the book rather than looping awkwardly around or over the book to the back. A number of chained libraries still survive in Europe. Figure 2-19 is a drawing of a bookcase from the Hereford Cathedral Library. The books are clearly shown shelved with the fore-edges and clasps facing forward, and most of their chains attached to the middle of one of the boards.

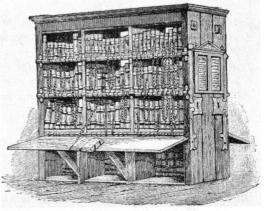

Figure 2-19 "Bookcase in the Chapter Library, Hereford Cathedral." John Willis Clark, *The Care of Books* (Cambridge, University Press, 1901), 175.

AN EXAMPLE FROM THE CARY COLLECTION

The Cary Collection preserves an example of a chained binding (Figure 2-20), though it is not from the medieval period, but rather from the 17th century. It is an edition of the works of John Gregory, printed in 1671, that was donated to Wells Cathedral in England on November 25, 1681.[58] This donation is recorded in a manuscript note on the book's front pastedown leaf (the paper

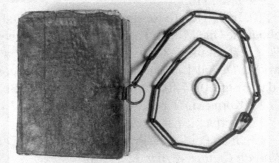

Figure 2-20 A chained bookbinding on John Gregory, *The works of the Reverend and Learned Mr. John Gregory* (London: Printed for Richard Royston, and Thomas Williams, 1671). RIT Cary Graphic Arts Collection.

attached to the inside of the front board). At some point after this date, the book was added to Wells Cathedral's chained library. Looking at the image, you can see how the chain is attached to a ring on the middle of the front board. The ring found on the other end of the chain once ran along a horizontal metal rod that ran parallel to the shelf the book rested on—ensuring that no reader could easily steal it. A book curse might also have helped.

NOTES

1. Dard Hunter, *Papermaking: The History and Technique of an Ancient Craft* (New York: Dover Publications, 1978), 52; Martyn Lyons, *Books: A Living History* (Los Angeles: J. Paul Getty Museum, 2011), 18, and J. S. Edgren, "China," in *A Companion to the History of the Book*, ed. Simon Eliot and Jonathan Rose (Malden, MA: Blackwell, 2007), 99.

2. Hunter, 5.

3. Lyons, 18; and Edgren, 97.

4. Edgren, 97.

5. Peter Kornicki, "Japan, Korea, and Vietnam," in *A Companion to the History of the Book*, ed. Simon Eliot and Jonathan Rose (Malden, MA: Blackwell, 2007), 111.

6. Special thanks to Yoshi Hill for identifying this block.

7. Kornicki, *The Book in Japan*, 113.

8. Kornicki, *The Book in Japan*, 116.

9. Ibid., 116.

10. Ibid., 116. To see an image of an original pagoda and to learn more about the One Million Pagodas, visit https://www.kyohaku.go.jp/eng/dictio/kouko/hyakuman.html. For a 3D model of a pagoda created by Cambridge Digital Library, see https://sketchfab.com/3d-models/hyakumanto-darani-fg8701-4-f0c76e17c0724b8b8e7f8dbf3b31cd26.

11. Kornicki, "Japan, Korea, and Vietnam," 111–112.

12. Kornicki, *The Book in Japan*, 115.

13. Sohn Pow-kee, "Printing since the 8th Century in Korea," *Koreana: Korean Culture & Arts* 32.2 (2018).

14. A book on the *Diamond Sutra* from the British Library notes this in its title: Frances Wood and Mark Barnard, *The Diamond Sutra: The Story of the World's Earliest Dated Printed Book* (London: British Library, 2010).

15. https://www.bl.uk/collection-items/the-diamond-sutra. This is an excellent spotlight on the *Diamond Sutra* on the British Library's website.

16. Edgren, 100.

17. Roberts and Skeat, 37.

18. Colin H. Roberts and T. C. Skeat, *The Birth of the Codex* (London; New York: Published for the British Academy by the Oxford University Press, 1983), 48.

19. Peter Stallybrass, "Books and Scrolls: Navigating the Bible," in *Books and Readers in Early Modern England: Material Studies,* ed. Jennifer Andersen and Elizabeth Sauer (Philadelphia: University of Pennsylvania Press, 2002), 43.

20. http://www.codexsinaiticus.org/en/codex.

21. "vellum, n.," OED Online, July 2018, Oxford University Press. http://www.oed.com.ezproxy.rit.edu/view/Entry/221992?redirectedFrom =vellum (accessed September 12, 2018).

22. See Raymond Clemens and Timothy Graham, *Introduction to Manuscript Studies* (Ithaca: Cornell University Press, 2007), 10, and Christopher De Hamel, *Scribes and Illuminators* (Toronto: University of Toronto Press, 1992), 11. For a video, see "How Parchment Is Made—Domesday—BBC Two," https://www.youtube.com/watch?v=2-SpLPFaRd0.

23. Sarah Fiddyment, Bruce Holsinger, Chiara Ruzzier, Alexander Devine, Annelise Binois, Umberto Albarella, Roman Fischer, et al., "Animal Origin of 13th-Century Uterine Vellum Revealed Using Noninvasive Peptide Fingerprinting," *Proceedings of the National Academy of Sciences of the United States of America* 112.49 (2015): 15066–15071, https://www.ncbi .nlm.nih.gov/pmc/articles/PMC4679014.

24. De Hamel, *Scribes*, 5–7; Derolez, 35.

25. Clemens and Graham, *Introduction*, 17; Derolez, 34–35.

26. Ibid., 22; Derolez, 31.

27. "In medieval illustrations, scribes are almost never depicted writing with their left hand," ibid., 18.

28. De Hamel, *Scribes,* 27.

29. A detailed demonstration of this process can be seen here: https:// youtu.be/u8LTei_AIs0.

30. De Hamel also makes this apt comparison, "Writing, like eating, was a two-handed operation," *Scribes,* 37.

31. Clemens and Graham, *Introduction*, 19–20, and De Hamel, *Scribes,* 32.

32. https://www.poetryfoundation.org/poems/44131/a-valediction-for bidding-mourning.

33. Jane Greenfield, *ABC of Bookbinding: A Unique Glossary with over 700 Illustrations for Collectors & Librarians* (New Castle, DE: Oak Knoll

Press; New York: Lyons Press, 1998), 33, and P. J. M. Marks, *The British Library Guide to Bookbinding: History and Techniques* (London: British Library, 1998), 39.

34. De Hamel, *Scribes and Illuminators*, 39.

35. Albert Derolez, *The Palaeography of Gothic Manuscript Books: From the Twelfth to the Early Sixteenth Century* (Cambridge, UK; New York: Cambridge University Press, 2003), 130.

36. Clemens and Graham, *Introduction*, 23.

37. De Hamel, *Scribes*, 7.

38. Ibid.

39. Clemens and Graham, *Introduction*, 23.

40. Leila Avrin, *Scribes, Scripts, and Books: The Book Arts from Antiquity to the Renaissance* (Chicago: American Library Association; London: The British Library, 1991), 224.

41. Margaret M. Smith, *The Title-Page, Its Early Development, 1460–1510* (New Castle, DE: Oak Knoll Press, 2000).

42. Rodericus Zamorensis, *Epistola de expugnatione Nigropontis* [Cologne: Ulrich Zel, about 1470–1471].

43. Clemens and Graham, *Introduction,* 14; Derolez, 33.

44. De Hamel, *Scribes*, 41; Clemens and Graham, *Introduction*, 49.

45. Derolez, 34.

46. J. A. Szirmai, *Archaeology of Medieval Bookbinding* (Aldershot, Hants; Brookfield, VT: Ashgate Publishing, 1999), 95.

47. De Hamel, *Scribes*, 67.

48. For an insightful article on book clasps, see J. Franklin Mowery, "Clasps, Schliessen, Clausuren: A Guide to the Manufacture and the Literature of Clasps," *Guild of Book Workers Journal* 24.2 (1991): 1–58.

49. Margit J. Smith, *The Medieval Girdle Book* (New Castle, DE: Oak Knoll Press, 2017), 9–11.

50. Roberts and Skeat, 17. Reviel Netz and William Noel, *The Archimedes Codex: How a Medieval Prayer Book Is Revealing the True Genius of Antiquity's Greatest Scientist* (Philadelphia: Da Capo Press, 2007), 121.

51. See Netz and Noel, and http://www.archimedespalimpsest.org/about.

52. *Origen, Operū Origenis Adamātii tomi duo priores*: cum tabula et indice generali p(ro)xime sequentibus (Paris: In edibus J. parvi et J. Badii Ascensii, 1519–1522).

53. https://folgerpedia.folger.edu/Recycled_Manuscripts. See also Christopher De Hamel, *Western Manuscripts and Miniatures: A Seventh-Century Insular Bifolium from Eusebins's Historia ecclesiastica* (London: Sotheby's, 1985).

54. Pedro de Ribadeneyra, *Leben Francisci Borgiae: dritten Generals der Societet Iesu* (Getruckt zu Ingolstatt: Durch Andream Angermayr, 1613).

55. Scott D. N. Cook, "Technological Revolutions and the Gutenberg Myth," in *Internet Dreams: Archetypes, Myths, and Metaphors*, ed. Mark Stefik (Cambridge, MA: MIT Press, 1997), 72.

56. Clemens, *Introduction*, 57. To view a Gothic coffer used to store and transport a book, see https://www.cabinet.ox.ac.uk/gothiccoffer and https://www.bodleian.ox.ac.uk/news/2019/jan-22.

57. Elmer D. Johnson, *History of Libraries in the Western World* (Metuchen, NJ: Scarecrow Press, 1970), 125. Johnson also notes, "A common word for library in the Middle Ages was armarium, which was literally the book-chest where the books were kept. The librarian, or person who supervised the books, was known as the armarius," 121.

58. John Gregory, *The Works of the Reverend and Learned Mr. John Gregory* (London: Printed for Richard Royston, and Thomas Williams, 1671).

FURTHER READING

Clemens, Raymond, and Timothy Graham. *Introduction to Manuscript Studies.* Ithaca, NY: Cornell University Press, 2007.

De Hamel, Christopher. *Scribes and Illuminators (Medieval Craftsmen).* Toronto: University of Toronto Press, 2009.

Derolez, Albert. *The Palaeography of Gothic Manuscript Books: From the Twelfth to the Early Sixteenth Century.* Cambridge, UK; New York: Cambridge University Press, 2003.

Edgren, J. S. "China." In *A Companion to the History of the Book*, edited by Simon Eliot and Jonathan Rose, 97–110. Malden, MA: Blackwell, 2007.

Gullick, Michael. "How Fast Scribes Write." In *Making the Medieval Book: Techniques of Production*, edited by Linda L. Brownrigg. Los Altos Hills, CA: Anderson-Lovelace, 1995.

Kornicki, Peter F. *The Book in Japan: A Cultural History from the Beginnings to the Nineteenth Century.* Leiden, Netherlands; Boston: Brill, 1998.

Kornicki, Peter F. "Japan, Korea, and Vietnam." In *A Companion to the History of the Book*, edited by Simon Eliot and Jonathan Rose, 111–125. Malden, MA: Blackwell, 2007.

Szirmai, J. A. *Archaeology of Medieval Bookbinding.* Aldershot, Hants, and Brookfield, VT: Ashgate Publishing, 1999.

THREE

Printing with Movable Type

Printing did not begin with Johannes Gutenberg in Germany in the 1450s. Printing was invented in China with the technology of woodblock printing in around the seventh century. As described in Chapter Two, text and images were carved in reverse and in relief onto blocks of wood. When a block was ready, it was inked, and paper was placed over the image. The impression was created by simple pressure printing. Printing with woodblocks had its drawbacks when producing longer texts. Carving text into a woodblock took a long time, much more so than the time it took to write it out by hand. Of course, the idea was that once you had created the woodblock, it could be reused to make multiple copies. Thus time was saved in the long run. If, however, any mistakes were introduced into the woodblock, they were difficult to fix. The block might even have to be recarved. This was a problem that needed to be solved.

The answer lay in movable characters, so that text could be set faster and mistakes could be more easily fixed. The evolution of movable type was a relatively slow one. It began in around 1040 CE in China when a man named Bì Shēng (c. 990–c. 1051) invented ceramic movable printing type, which he set in an iron tray to print. Clay, however, was a fragile material for printing, even when used with pressure printing. Stronger materials were needed. About a century later, movable *wood* type was introduced. By the early 13th century, movable *metal* type was being manufactured.

Scholars trace the casting of bronze printing type to 1234 CE on Kang-wha (Ganghwa) Island in South Korea.[1] Historical records suggest that the type was cast to print copies of *Sangjong kogum yemun*, a multivolume book of ceremonies and etiquette. Sand casting was the technology used to make the type, as recorded in the 15th century by the scholar Song Hyon:

> At first, one cuts letters in beech wood. One fills a trough level with fine sandy [clay] of the reed-growing seashore. Wood-cut letters are pressed into the sand, then the impressions become negative and form letters [molds]. At this step, placing one trough together with another, one pours the molten bronze down into an opening. The fluid flows in, filing these negative molds, one by one becoming type. Lastly, one scrapes and files off the irregularities, and piles them up to be arranged.[2]

This method of casting type evolved out of the techniques for producing coins.[3] Two centuries later, a similar repurposing of technologies used for casting objects like coins for casting printing type would take place in Europe.

Although there is a surviving record of *Sangjong kogum yemun* being printed with metal type, no copies of the volumes survive. The oldest surviving book printed with metal movable type was produced in Korea in 1377.[4] It is the *Chikchi Simch'e yojol* or "the selected teaching of the Buddhist masters." This book is preserved in the Bibliothèque Nationale in Paris, France. As noted by Professor Ch'on Hye-bong, the type used was set in a galley of 11 columns that held about 18–20 characters.[5]

The Cary Collection preserves two pieces of metal printing type cast in the 15th century in Korea or China, figure 3-1. They were a part of the collection acquired by the library from the former New York Times Museum of the Recorded Word. Although they are among the smallest artifacts held in the library, they are among the most profound, as they make a direct connection to some the earliest printing with metal movable type. The type are the characters for "peace" and "sky."

Figure 3-1   Printing type, Korea or China, 15th century. RIT Cary Graphic Arts Collection. Photograph by Elizabeth Lamark.

JOHANNES GUTENBERG

While printing with movable type was invented by Bì Shēng in China in the 11th century, it was popularized in Europe in the mid-15th century. The pivotal figure was Johannes Gutenberg (1397–1468). Several contemporary documents survive documenting the life of Gutenberg, as well as acknowledging his invention of printing with movable type with a press.[6] Gutenberg collaborated with two associates: Johann Fust (1400–1466) and Peter Schöffer (c. 1425–c. 1502), a capitalist and scribe, respectively, who both continued to be important figures in the development of printing. Gutenberg was a goldsmith—he was identified as such in a document from 1444—and thus he understood the technologies of casting metal pieces that featured text and images such as jewelry or coins.[7] He would also have been familiar with another technology of the period—wooden presses used for making wine from grapes or olive oil from olives. How Gutenberg thought to combine these two technologies into one that would revolutionize printing is unclear—not enough documentation of this history survives. Nevertheless, the invention is a dramatic example of repurposing existing technologies to create a new technology.

Gutenberg was a businessman. One of his financial ventures in the 1470s, before he turned to printing, was the production of pilgrim mirrors. At the time, Europeans were taking part in pilgrimages to holy sites, where they would view saints' relics. Throngs of people often gathered in front of these artifacts. Having a mirror to hold up high over one's head could help make viewing the relics possible. It was also believed that the mirror captured some of the relics' holy essence. Some scholars see some connection between the technologies Gutenberg used for mass-producing mirrors with the technologies he later used for casting type and printing on a wooden press.[8] At the very least, Gutenberg, as a businessman, saw an opportunity or need for increasing the production and sale of books.

TYPEFOUNDING

Building on existing technologies for metal casting, Gutenberg developed a method of casting movable printing type. Scholars believe that he used a hand mold similar to the one shown in figure 3-2. The process of typefounding began with punchcutting, that is, hand carving in relief each letter of the alphabet in upper and lower case, along with all other characters and punctuation required, onto the ends of steel punches. Each punch

Figure 3-2   A hand mold used to cast type. RIT Cary Graphic Arts Collection. Photograph by Elizabeth Lamark.

was then carefully driven into a small, copper block, leaving an impression of the letter. This created a matrix or casting mold for each character. The matrix was then inserted into a hand mold in such a way that the recessed area of the matrix rested at the end of a channel. Into this channel was poured a molten alloy of lead, tin, and antimony. In Asia, the metals used for casting type had been iron and bronze. As Marcou rightly notes, "mixtures of lead, was another of Gutenberg's contributions to the history of printing."[9]

The typefounder then dipped a ladle into a pot of this molten metal mixture and quickly poured it into the funneled opening of the mold. The

Figure 3-3   A punch, matrix, and piece of type. RIT Cary Graphic Arts Collection. Photograph by Elizabeth Lamark.

metal hardened quickly, so to help the metal move quickly though the channel and down into the impression in the matrix, the type founder jerked the mold upward while pouring. The casting produced a rectangular piece of type with a character in reverse at its tip. Attached to the newly cast type was excess metal that had filled the channel behind it. This excess metal was called the jet. The typefounder snapped the jet off of the type and returned it back to the pot of molten metal. Figure 3-3 shows a punch and a matrix used to cast a musical half note, and the resulting piece of type.

In this manner, the typefounder produced a number of type characters for each letter, depending on how frequently each letter was typically used. A large number of Es, for example, were cast, as opposed to a relatively smaller number of Zs. Each piece of type was smoothed on a polishing stone and distributed into a type case. A full set of printing type characters for each particular typeface design and size is called a fount.

Figure 3-4 is a modern painting by Robert A. Thom of Gutenberg casting type. Gutenberg holds a hand mold into which he pours molten metal with a ladle. Below him are piles of type that he has already cast and a pot of molten metal heated by a furnace. A polishing stone rests on a stand in the lower right foreground. Behind Gutenberg, another man distributes type into type cases.

Figure 3-4   Robert A. Thom, *Johann Gutenberg and Moveable Type*, oil on canvas, 48 × 36 inches, Kimberly Clark Graphic Communications Through the Ages Series, c. 1966. RIT Cary Graphic Arts Collection.

42-LINE BIBLE

Gutenberg's first printed works appeared in the early 1450s. Working with associates Fust and Schöffer, their endeavors began with shorter works, such as Donatus's Latin grammar and indulgences.[10] Both of these publications were genres well-served by the multiplying technology of printing. Latin grammars were popular texts used in schools. Indulgences were contracts designed to be completed by hand that forgave sins after recitation of prayer or financial contribution to the church.

Gutenberg's greatest accomplishment was, of course, printing copies of the Latin Vulgate Bible. Printed in approximately 1455, the Gutenberg Bible, also known as the 42-Line Bible, was the first major book printed in Europe with metal movable type. As with manuscript Bibles of the same period, the printed Bible was a large undertaking of 1,282 pages that likely took several years to complete. The print run of Gutenberg's Bible is estimated at between 158 and 180 copies,[11] of which 49 copies survive (if fragments are included, the number of copies is 64).[12]

In terms of the appearance of his printed Bible, Gutenberg looked to manuscript Bibles for inspiration. This was a natural choice. In the history of technology, new media often imitate and build on the media that came before. Printed books imitated manuscripts. Thus, on the left of figure 3-5 is a leaf from the Gutenberg Bible and on the right is a leaf from a mid-15th-century German *manuscript* Missal (a liturgical book used during mass). When teaching printing history in the Cary Collection, my colleagues and I often show these two leaves to students and ask which is printed and which is written by hand. The students usually guess correctly, noticing the manuscript's ruled page or its ragged right margin—as opposed to the printed page's justified right margin. The question is admittedly a trick question, because the Gutenberg Bible is, in fact, a hybrid production. The text in black was printed, but space was left for manuscript ornamentation such as decorative initial letters. In this way, printing-house practices in Gutenberg's shop followed a similar division of labor found in the production of manuscripts. In a scriptorium, a scribe would write out the main body of text and the illuminator would provide any decoration. In the earliest printing houses, the printer printed the text, and an illuminator filled in the decorative elements. This hybridity in printed books that began with Gutenberg lasted for about 50 years, after which elements such as woodcut initial letters and illustrations replace decorative matter supplied by hand.

When viewing the printed Gutenberg leaf next to a manuscript leaf, some students remark on the similarity between the printed text and the

Figure 3-5 A leaf from a Gutenberg Bible, Mainz, Germany, c. 1455 (left) and a leaf from a 15th-century manuscript Missal (right). RIT Cary Graphic Arts Collection.

manuscript. This is because the blackletter or gothic type imitates the blackletter or gothic handwriting characteristic of that period. Indeed, early type is always imitating handwriting. The primary handwriting style found in Germany during Gutenberg's time was blackletter. In Italy, humanist handwriting had evolved away from blackletter and returned to earlier more rounded letterforms. In the decades following Gutenberg's advances in printing, humanist handwriting would inspire the casting of roman and italic typeface designs that would eventually all but replace blackletter styles in Europe.

THE HAND PRESS

The type of printing press used from Gutenberg in the 1450s to about the early 1800s was the wooden common hand press. This technology was an adaptation of wooden screw presses used in the production of wine and olive oil. Generally, when using this sort of press, a bar was pulled, turning a screw that caused a rectangular wooden plate or "platen" to press downward with considerable force. Rather than pressing grapes into wine, or olives into olive oil, the wooden common hand press pushed dampened paper onto inked type, making a printed impression in the paper. The functions of a printing press are best learned through live demonstrations. Readers are encouraged to visit a local book arts center, or museum or library that might offer workshops or demonstrations using a printing press. There are also many videos of printing presses in action to be found online.

PRINTING ON A HAND PRESS

The process of printing on a hand press began with a compositor pulling type housed in wooden type cases and setting it as lines of text in a composing stick. In the early days of printing, two cases held a full supply or fount of type. This is the original use of the word "fount" or "font" in printing—a full set of characters of one typeface in one size. The word "font" today has come to also mean typeface, or design of the letters. Physically, a fount was housed in two type cases: the uppercase and lowercase. The upper held majuscule or capital letters, the lower held the miniscule letters. In this way, we get our terms "uppercase" and "lowercase" from the physical location of majuscule and miniscule letters in type cases.

Type cases evolved from being housed in two cases to being housed in one that contained both uppercase and lowercase letters. The most common modern layout in the United States is the California job case, figure 3-6. Each compartment houses a specific letter, number, punctuation, or spacing of various widths. The size of each compartment is relative to the quantity of type needed for that character. For example, in the California job case, the compartment for the lowercase letter e is the largest because in English e is the most frequently used character. The compartment for the lowercase q, on the other hand, is quite small, because the letter q is less frequently needed in English. In French type cases, however, the compartment for q would be larger, and compartments would be needed for accented letters. So the organization of type cases also varies by language.

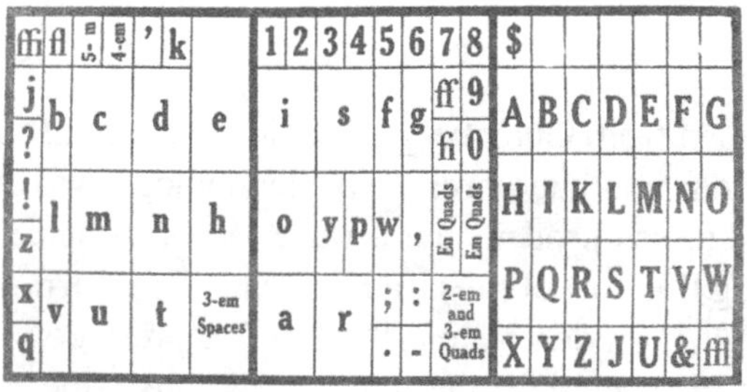

Figure 3-6   Layout of a California job case. Printed by Amelia Fontanel.

As noted above, the compositor pulled type from the cases and set it in a composing stick like the one shown in figure 3-7 with a line of type that reads "Media Archaeology." Typically, compositors held the wooden or metal composing stick in their left hand while pulling type with their right hand. Compositors placed the type in the stick upside down and left to right, using their thumb to hold the type in place. While reading letters upside down and backward might sound daunting, it is a skill that is not too diffi-

Figure 3-7 Composing stick with a line of type set. RIT Cary Graphic Arts Collection.

cult to pick up through hands-on experience. Also, to help ensure that the type is placed properly in the composing stick, each piece of type was marked with a nick (or groove) on the bottom side of the shank. When type is set correctly in a composing stick, the nicks face up and are visible. Thus a line of type should create a visible line of nicks. The compositor also might feel the nick, or lack of a nick, with his or her thumbs. This helps correctly set letters that are similar to others when upside down. Frequent offenders include lowercase U and N, and lowercase P and Q.

The process of setting type in a composing stick progressed letter by letter, word by word, sentence by sentence. Leading, thin horizontal spacing material made of lead, was usually set between the lines of type. Once the stick was full, the type was transferred to a wooden, and later metal tray called a galley. This process was repeated until the galley tray had a full page or pages of text. The type was then transferred into an iron frame called a chase. Within the chase the printer assembles a forme—bodies of type and illustrative matter constituting a page or pages of text, depending on the book format being printed. Empty space in the forme between the type and the sides of the chase frame was filled in using wooden or metal blocks called furniture. Furniture was not the same height as the type, but shorter so that it would not take on ink (since that would result in its transfer to the paper while printing). The type and furniture were tightened or "locked up" in the forme using quoins—short wood wedges that were hammered between the furniture and the sides and bottoms of the chase to apply pressure and hold everything firmly in place. In later printing, quoins were made of metal and could be adjusted mechanically using a key to tighten or loosen the forme.

Once the forme was assembled, it was lifted and moved to the bed of the printing press. If perchance bad fortune befell the printer and he or she did not lock up the forme properly, moving the loose form could cause the type to fall out, negating hours of hard work in one loud cascade of lead. This printing mishap is called "pieing" the type. In his autobiography,

Benjamin Franklin describes such an incident in his shop and how his overcoming of the accident demonstrated his industrious nature:

> But so determin'd I was to continue doing a Sheet a Day of the Folio, that one Night, when having impos'd my Forms, I thought my Day's Work over, one of them by accident was broken and two Pages reduc'd to Pie, I immediately distributed and compos'd it over again before I went to bed. And this Industry visible to our Neighbours began to give us Character and Credit.[13]

Figure 3-8 is an illustrated diagram of a reproduction wooden hand press designed and produced by students at RIT in 2016.[14] Hand presses were operated as follows: the forme holding type, furniture, and any illustrative matter in the form of borders, initial letters, or woodcut illustrations was set onto the press stone, which rested in the carriage or coffin. Two press operators worked the press. One press operator, called the beater, used ink balls (balls of wool wrapped in leather on wooden handles) to pick up ink from the ink-block (the flat surface onto which the ink was spread) and apply the ink onto the type. Printer's ink was thicker, that is, more viscous than the writing ink used with a quill. It was usually made using linseed oil as the vehicle and lampblack as the pigment.

The second press operator, called the puller, placed a sheet of paper onto the tympan. The tympan consisted of a wooden frame around which parchment was pulled tight (think of a tight drum—"tympani"). Sheets of paper were usually dampened before printing. This helped soften the paper so it would take the impression more readily. Paper was held onto the tympan by small pins called points. The puller then lowered the frisket down over the tympan. Attached to the tympan, the frisket was a second frame that helped hold the paper in place. The frisket was also wrapped in parchment; however, a window was cut out, exposing only the portion of the paper meant to receive the impression. This prevented any stray ink that might be on the furniture from getting onto the paper.

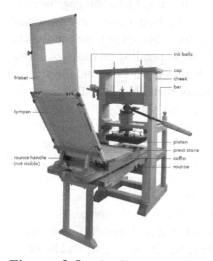

Figure 3-8 A diagram of a wooden common press. Illustration by Blayke Morrow.

The puller lowered the tympan and frisket over the forme in the carriage, so that the paper hovered millimeters above the inked type. The puller then turned the handle of the rounce (or crank), which moved the carriage (and with it the forme, frisket, and tympan) under the platen. The puller pulled the bar (or devil's arm), which turned the screw and, in turn, pushed the wooden platen down onto the back of the tympan. This pressed the paper onto the inked type with considerable pressure. This was how the printed impression was made. The platen of a wooden common press was not large enough to make an impression over the whole sheet of paper. So, after the first pull of the press, the puller turned the rounce handle again, and moved the carriage further under the platen and took a second impression from the rest of the type in the forme.

After the full impression had been made, the puller performed the same operation in reverse. He turned the rounce handle, recalling the carriage back from under the platen. He lifted the tympan and frisket and removed the printed sheet of paper. As this was happening, the beater could make a quick study of the impression on the paper to make note of any place where the application of ink might have been too light or heavy, and make any adjustments while re-inking the type. The puller then hung the sheet to dry on a line. Further along in the history of printing, the paper might be laid to dry on a rack.

Figure 3-9 is a modern depiction of a young Benjamin Franklin working in his printing shop. The painting accurately shows how two press operators operated a hand press. In this painting, Franklin, the puller, is operating the bar, while his beater holds the ink balls.[15] In the lower right corner of the painting, there is a stack of damped paper ready for the press. This pile was sometimes called the heap. Note how the printed sheets are hung up to dry. Also note that they have been printing eight pages to a sheet or "eight up." Printing both sides of the sheet in this format produces 16 pages. This format, as discussed below, is called an octavo. Note also the stands of type shown at the left of the painting and their upper and lower cases.

So how long did all of this take? What was the daily output of a common press?

A lot depended on the skill and speed of the compositors and press operators—some were faster than others. According to Gaskell,

The token of 250 sheets printed on one side was conventionally called an hour's work, but this figure was at best a mean. . . . In fact the rate of work achieved was usually less than 250 impressions per hour, or 3,000 impressions per 12-hour day, though it is impossible to generalize further.[16]

Figure 3-9   Robert A. Thom, *Benjamin Franklin*, oil on canvas, 32 × 24 inches, Kimberly Clark Graphic Communications Through the Ages Series, c. 1966. RIT Cary Graphic Arts Collection.

How many copies of one edition were printed? That often depended on the texts being printed, as well as the capacity of the printing house. Surviving evidence of print runs from the incunabula period (the first 50 years of printing in Europe) show numbers ranging from 300 to 800 copies.[17] According to Gaskell, from the 16th century through the late 18th century, editions generally numbered "1,000 to 1,500 copies."[18]

PAPER

While parchment was the principal writing surface throughout the Middle Ages, paper found increased use for manuscripts during the 14th century.[19] From this period up through about the 19th century, paper was "laid paper" made from linen rags. Material such as old cloth rags were fermented over a period of time so they could be macerated, added to a vat of water, and beat into pulp. The papermaker took a mold and deckle, which were essentially a wire screen and wooden frame that held it within, and dipped them into the

Figure 3-10   George I. Parrish, Jr., *Papermaking at Fabriano*, oil on canvas, 35 × 26 inches, Kimberly Clark Graphic Communications Through the Ages Series, c. 1966. RIT Cary Graphic Arts Collection.

vat. As the papermaker lifted the mold out of the vat, he shook it so that the pulp spread evenly on the frame and excess water drained out through the screen. The paper dried on the screen and was then stacked within felts to dry further. The paper was pressed and finished. Figure 3-10 is modern painting depicting the various stages of papermaking. The setting is a paper mill in Fabriano, Italy, an important center for papermaking beginning in the Middle Ages. Beginning with the Gutenberg Bible, paper was most often used for this new technology of the hand press. Parchment was used occasionally in early printing (and thereafter for rare, special editions).

BOOK FORMATS AND SIZES

The format of a book is determined by how many times the printed sheet of paper is folded. The most common book formats from the hand press period are the broadside, folio, quarto, and octavo. A broadside is an unfolded printed sheet with text on one or both sides. This produces

Figure 3-11 Books in folio, quarto, and octavo (l-r). RIT Cary Graphic Arts Collection.

something akin to a modern poster. A folio is a sheet folded once, producing two leaves or four pages. A quarto is a sheet folded twice, producing four leaves or eight pages. An octavo is a sheet folded three times, producing eight leaves or 16 pages. Figure 3-11 shows each of the three book formats. Figure 3-12 provides diagrams of how each of these three common formats (as well as the 16mo) are folded from one sheet. There are many different ways to fold a sheet—thus there are many formats of books.

Format is *not* synonymous with size. The format of a book might factor in its size, but size relates primarily to the size of the sheet of paper that has been printed on. Although folios are typically larger than quartos, for example, a quarto produced from large sheets of paper might be larger than a folio produced from smaller sheets of paper. Due to the folding, folios and octavos tend to be more rectangular; quartos tend to be more squarish. Sometimes, you might initially deduce whether a book is a folio, quarto, or octavo by its size and shape, as shown in figure 3-11, but format always needs to be confirmed bibliographically.

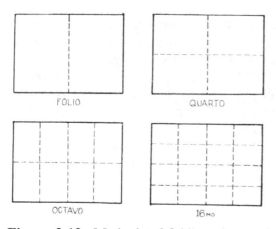

Figure 3-12 Methods of folding sheets of paper. Florence O. Bean and John C. Brodhead, *Bookbinding for Beginners* (Boston, Mass.: School Arts Pub. Co., 1914). 66.

Identifying the format of a book is properly done by examining the chain lines and watermarks in the paper. Chain lines and watermarks are marks made on laid paper during its production as it rests in the mold and deckle. Chain lines are the widely spaced lines running parallel across the paper sheet. A watermark is a design fashioned by manipulating the wire in the mold. Watermarks often identify the papermaker and the size of the paper. Usually, they are not visible to the eye until revealed by a light source held behind the paper. This is safely done by using a cold light pad that can be carefully placed behind a leaf (most rare book libraries will have one for readers to use). In a pinch, one can briefly and very carefully shine a flashlight behind the leaf. The direction of the chain lines and the position of the watermark should determine the format of a book. In a folio, the chain lines run vertically and the

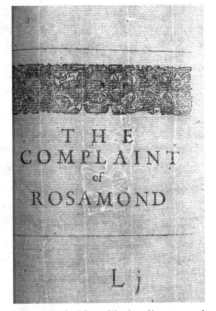

Figure 3-13 Chain lines and a watermark are revealed using a light pad. Photo by Annie Immediata.

watermark is found in the center of the leaf. In a quarto, the chain lines run horizontally and the watermark is found in the center of the spine fold or gutter. In an octavo, the chain lines run vertically and the watermark is found in the upper gutter. Figure 3-13 shows the chain lines and a unicorn watermark found in a 1602 folio edition of *The Works of Samuel Daniel*.

Like manuscript books, printed books came in a variety of sizes for a variety of readers—its size indicating how it was probably used. A large folio like the one at the left in figure 3-11 is not the sort of book a reader would want to carry around, or read casually in a chair or while lounging outside. A reader could realistically only comfortably read a book of its size using a lectern or on a table. Large folio books might not have been intended for use by a single person, but rather may have been designed to be read by several people at a time. They might have been intended to be more of a public book than a private book—something to be shared. A smaller octavo book like the one at the lower right in figure 3-11 is clearly designed to be more of a handheld book. You could read a book of this size wherever you want. It is larger than the size of cuneiform tablet and nearly the same size as a wax tablet. This is a book that a reader could stuff in his or her pocket and carry. It is perhaps a personal book meant for one reader.

PRINTING SMALLER FORMATS

The figure who had a profound influence on the printing of smaller format books was the Venetian printer Aldus Manutius (1449/50–1515). Aldus popularized printing popular works in the octavo form. In April 1501, he began publishing a series of classical works in octavo with an edition of Virgil's *Aeneid*. A month later in May he released his second pocket-sized book, an edition of the works of the Roman poet Horace, figure 3-14. As scholar Martin Davies writes, "The innovation lay not in the small format, often used by printers for devotional texts, but in applying it to a class of literature hitherto issued in large and imposing folios or quartos."[20] In this way, Aldus used the octavo format for works that had normally appeared in large formats. That trend caught on. In England, one of the printers responsible for popularizing smaller format books was Wynken de Worde (died 1534), especially "the quarto size de Worde found so profitable in the fields of romance and schoolbooks."[21] Wynken de Worde was apprentice to William Caxton, who introduced printing to England in 1475 or 1476. Caxton is known for choosing to print books in the English language—one of the very first books he printed in England was Chaucer's *Canterbury Tales* (c. 1477). It was Caxton's successor, Wynken de Worde, who first took advantage of the marketability of books produced in smaller formats. In particular, de Worde mass-produced contemporary religious works and schoolbooks in cheaper quarto and octavo formats, reserving the folio format for major titles such as Sir Thomas Malory's *Morte D'arthur* (1498).

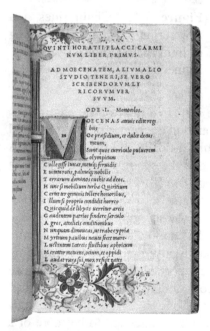

Figure 3-14 The opening of Horace, *Horativs* (Venice: Aldus Manutius, 1501). RIT Cary Graphic Arts Collection.

The choice of whether to print a book in folio, quarto, or octavo (to revisit the most common formats) was ultimately a practical one. From the point of view of the stationer putting up the capital, all publications posed a financial risk; folios, however, were typically a more expensive proposition. Paper was the chief determinant of the cost of producing a book, and stationers had to acquire stocks of paper before printing began. Because folio books usually required more paper, the stationer (in most cases the printer himself) had to invest a significant amount of money up front.[22] Needless to say, the folio was not the size for the mass market. Thus, hand-held printed books really came into style in the beginning of the 16th century and have remained popular ever since. Something like Aldus's editions of Virgil and Horace can be seen as descendants of cuneiform and wax tablets, while predecessors to the modern paperback book.

GATHERING THE LEAVES

The quires or gatherings of a printed folio (sheets folded once) are gathered and nested together in the same manner as quires of a manuscript book. In the case of a quarto, double-folded sheets produce quires that are stacked on top of each other or nested together to create the text block. Octavo quires are stacked or nested in a similar manner. In order to ensure that the quires are gathered in the correct order, printed books used methods similar to those used in manuscript books. A catchword printed at the bottom right of the page, beneath the body of text, matched the word that appeared first on the subsequent page. This helped ensure the text followed the right order, both when setting the type and when folding and gathering the printed sheets. Printed books also used signatures in a manner similar to their use in manuscript books. Each leaf of a printed book typically was labeled in the lower righthand corner of the recto page with a number and letter combination. For a folio with gatherings of six leaves, for example, the leaves of the first gathering would be labeled with the signatures a1, a2, a3, and a4 (the remaining a5 and a6 were often left blank but understood). The leaves of the second gathering would be labeled b1, b2, b3, and b4 (with b5 and b6 left blank). And so on.

BINDING

Up until the late 17th century or so, books were more often sold unbound. If book owners wanted their books bound, they took them to bookbinders after purchasing them. The techniques of bookbinding in the first centuries of the printed book in Europe were much like those practiced in the Middle Ages as described in Chapter Two. Once the sheets were gathered into a text block, they were sewn together and onto several sewing supports. Boards made of wood or pasteboard were attached to the text block using the extended ends of the sewing supports. As with the bindings of manuscript books, the covering material used in binding was invariably prepared from the skins of domestic livestock. Usually, this was leather prepared from calf, goat, sheep, or pig hides. Parchment was also a binding option.

Sometimes book owners might have chosen to bind several of their books together in one volume. The books chosen need not have been written by the same author, though they could be. They often were collections of related subjects such as religious sermons or playtexts. Such volumes are called sammelbands ("bound-withs" is another term that might be used, especially in libraries). Sammelbands are important documents in the history of the book. When they survive without having been later broken up into their individual, stand-alone volumes, they present to us miniature libraries providing evidence into the collecting habits of their former owners.

INCUNABULA

Books produced in the first 50 years or so of printing in Europe are called incunabula, a Latin term meaning "from the cradle" or "in swaddling clothing."[23] Incunabula are defined as books printed prior to 1501. These are printed books in their infancy—the firsts of their kind in the West. The evolution of incunabula through these first decades (and well into the 16th century) shows how the form of the printed book developed gradually. At the most basic level, printed books imitated manuscript books—in a way, of course, manuscript books were the only medium for printing to imitate. Thus, the first features of printed books were very much like their manuscript counterparts. We saw already how Gutenberg followed the design paradigms and workflow of scribes and left spaces on the printed page for additional decorative embellishment. This certainly continues through the incunabula period and beyond. In this way, incunabula were often hybrids of manuscript and print.

Figure 3-15 is a page from Aulus Gellius's *Noctes Atticae* (Attic Nights), printed in Venice by Nicolas Jenson (c. 1420–c. 1480) in 1472, held in the Cary Collection. Gellius was a first-century Roman grammarian, and his *Attic Nights* was a popular commonplace book with thoughts and notes on a variety of subjects. In the Cary Collection's copy of Jenson's edition, the spaces left by the printer for decorative initial letters were not embellished at the time. Unfortunately, on this particular page, a later reader rather roughly supplied the missing letter p. Also note the lack of pagination on this page. Page numbers would be a feature that would develop in time, preceded by foliation—or the numbering of each leaf (every recto, or right-hand page). Jenson's edition of *Attic Nights* has no title page. Medieval manuscripts seldom had title pages and, similarly, early books did not either. Like manuscripts, the text of printed books might also begin with an *incipit* ("it begins"). To protect the first page of text, printers placed a blank leaf in front of it. As Margaret M. Smith documents in her book *The Title-Page, Its Early Development 1460–1510*, the protective blank would soon have a printed label title used to identify the text that followed.[24] Decorative elements such as woodcut illustrations soon joined the label title.[25] After a while, printers then saw the benefit of using the once blank leaf to further advertise the book, so they started putting information on it such as the author, title, and publisher. The presentation of this information grew more elaborate and decorative. In this way, the title page was born. Smith connects all of these roles of the title page, that is, "protection, identification, and advertising" to "new needs brought with the advent of mass production."[26]

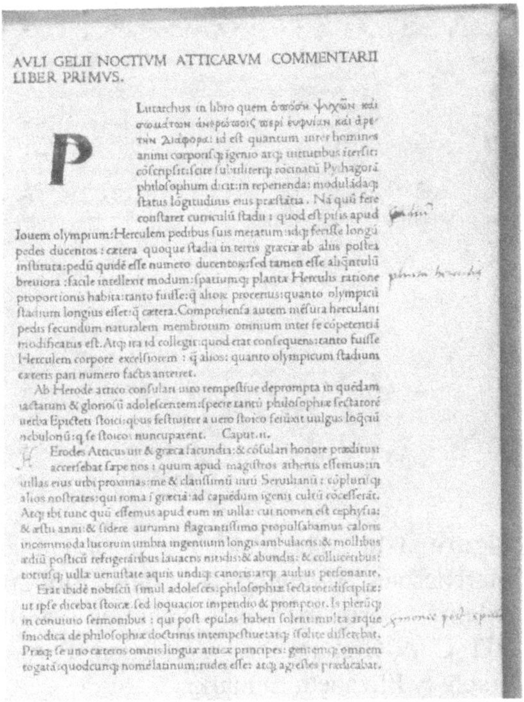
AVLI GELII NOCTIVM ATTICARVM COMMENTARII
LIBER PRIMVS.

P Lutarchus in libro quem ὁπόση ψυχῶν καὶ
σωμάτων ἀνθρώποις περὶ εὐφυίαν καὶ ἀρε-
τὴν διαφορά: id est quantum inter homines
animi corporisq; ingenio atq; uirtutibus intersit:
cōscripsit: scite subtiliterq; ratiocinatū Pythagorā
philosophum dicit: in reperienda: modulandaq;
status lōgitudinis eius præstātia. Nā quū fere
constaret curriculū stadii: quod est pisis apud
Iouem olympium: Herculem pedibus suis metatum: idq; fecisse longū
pedes ducentos: cætera quoque stadia in terris græciæ ab aliis postea
instituta: pedū quidē esse numero ducentorū: sed tamen esse aliq̄ntulū
breuiora: facile intellexit modum: spatiumq; plantæ Herculis ratione
proportionis habita: tanto fuisse: q̄ aliorū procerius: quanto olympicū
stadium longius esset: q̄ cætera. Comprehensa autem mēsura herculani
pedis secundum naturalem membrorum omnium inter se cōpetentiā
modificatus est. Atq; ita id collegit: quod erat consequens: tanto fuisse
Herculem corpore excelsiorem: q̄ alios: quanto olympicum stadium
cæteris pari numero factis anteiret.
Ab Herode attico consulari uiro tempestiue deprompta in quēdam
iactantem & gloriosū adolescentem: specie tantū philosophiæ sectatorē
uerba Epicteti stoici: quibus festiuiter a uero stoico seiūxit uulgus loq̄ciū
nebulonū: q se stoicos nuncuparent. Caput. ii.
H Erodes Atticus uir & græca facundia: & cōsulari honore præditus:
accersebat sæpe nos: quum apud magistros athenis essemus: in
uillas eius urbi proximas: me & clarissimū uirū Seruilianū: cōpluresq;
alios nostrates: qui roma ī græciā: ad capiēdum ingenii cultū cōcesserāt.
Atq; ibi tunc quū essemus apud eum in uilla: cui nomen est cephysia:
& æstu anni: & sidere autumni flagrantissimo propulsabamus caloris
incommoda lucorum umbra ingentium longis ambulacris: & mollibus
ædiū posticū refrigerātibus lauacris nitidis: & abundis: & collucētibus:
totiusq; uillæ uenustate aquis undiq; canoris: atq; auibus personante.
Erat ibidē nobiscū simul adolescēs: philosophiæ sectator: disciplinæ:
ut ipse dicebat stoicæ: sed loquacior impendio & promptior. Is plerūq;
in conuiuio sermonibus: qui post epulas haberi solent: multa atque
immodica de philosophiæ doctrinis intempestiue: atq; īsolite disserebat.
Præq; se uno cæteros omnis linguæ atticæ principes: gentemq; omnem
togatā: quodcunq; nomē latinum: rudes esse: atq; agrestes prædicabat.

Figure 3-15 Space left for an initial letter in Aulus Gellius, *Noctes Atticae* (Venice: Nicolaus Jenson, 1472). RIT Cary Graphic Arts Collection.

In incunabula, the information regarding the text, who printed it, and where and when, usually appeared at the very end of the book in a colophon. As we have seen, the use of a colophon dates back to cuneiform tablets. More directly, it is a continuation of the use of an explicit in manuscript books. Figure 3-16 shows an early colophon in a copy of *Mammotrectus*

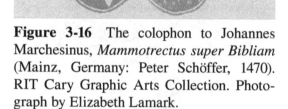

Figure 3-16 The colophon to Johannes Marchesinus, *Mammotrectus super Bibliam* (Mainz, Germany: Peter Schöffer, 1470). RIT Cary Graphic Arts Collection. Photograph by Elizabeth Lamark.

super Bibliam (Nourish upon the Bible) dating to 1470 and printed by Peter Schöffer, who had once worked with Gutenberg. This colophon begins "Explicit" or "here ends" and provides the title of the book and names Schöffer as the printer. It even notes that he finished his work happily or "feliciter." This bibliographic information (author, title, place, publisher, year) is still the essential information cited when we reference a book. As books evolved, this information moved from the colophon to the title page. The illustration included in the colophon to *Mammotrectus super Bibliam* displays the coats of arms of both Schöffer and his former partner Johann Fust. This is a printer's device or mark—a logo used to identify the printer. This graphic element in early printed books would also later move to the title page.

STORAGE

The invention of the printing press facilitated the production of books on a large scale. As books became increasingly available and more affordable, the size of book collections increased for institutions and individuals with the means to afford books. As the sizes of libraries grew, books were stored on shelves, much in the same manner as they are housed on shelves today. There were differences, however. Rather than shelved vertically, as has become the accustomed manner, books were often stacked horizontally. If one owned only a few books, then one would not need the space afforded by shelving books vertically. As collections continued to grow, shelving books vertically became a more common practice. Books were also usually shelved with their fore-edges (the paper edges) facing outward rather than their spines. Because of this, early printed books might have titles and/or authors written on their fore-edge. Figure 3-17, for example, shows an edition of Plutarch's *Lives* from 1553 held at the Cary Collection. An abbreviated title reading "Plutarchi Illustri Vitae" or "The Lives of the Illustrious Plutarch" appears at the top of this book's fore-edge, suggesting that it once stood vertically on a shelf with its fore-edge out.

Figure 3-17   An early owner inscribed the title of this book on its fore-edge. *Plutarch, Plutarchi cheronei Græcorum Romanorumque illustrium vitae* (Basileae: Apud Mich. Isingrinium, 1553). RIT Cary Graphic Arts Collection. Photograph by Elizabeth Lamark.

Images from the 16th century that show books in their natural habitats often depict them on shelves resting both horizontally and vertically with their fore-edges out. Moving forward in time, such images begin to reflect changes in how books were stored. In the case of Johann Amos Comenius's *Orbis sensualium pictus* (*The Visible World in Pictures*), earlier and later editions illustrate a change in bibliographic fashion.[27] A schoolbook that uses illustrations to teach Latin vocabulary, *Orbis sensualium pictus* first appeared in print in 1659 and went through numerous editions through the 18th century. The woodcut image depicting a "Study" found in the earlier editions shows books shelved vertically with their fore-edges out, figure 3-18. Later 18th-century editions of *Orbis sensualium pictus* show that the book's original illustrations have been

Figure 3-18   Johann Amos Comenius, *Joh. Amos Commenii orbis sensualium pictus* (London: John Sprint, 1705). RIT Cary Graphic Arts Collection. Photograph by Amelia Fontanel.

Figure 3-19   Johann Amos Comenius, *Joh. Amos Commenii orbis sensualium pictus* (London: Printed for S. Leacroft, 1777). RIT Cary Graphic Arts Collection. Photograph by Amelia Fontanel.

redone. The image of the study was updated to show books on shelves with their spines facing outward, figure 3-19. During the time between the early editions of the book and those from the 18th century, bibliographic fashions had clearly changed.

PROVENANCE

Readers often leave traces behind in books that provide evidence of how they used and cared for them. If books are examined in detail, it can be possible to trace the ownership of a book back to when it was first printed and deduce aspects of the book's life. Since the earliest years of printing, readers have made a habit of signing their names in books that they owned. Some even date their signature or augment it with "his book" or "her book." Such inscriptions identify former owners. Book owners might also paste a printed bookplate into their book to identify themselves or their family as the owners. The design of a bookplate might range from a modest slip simply presenting the owner's names (sometimes called a book label) to an elaborate illustration that might depict a scene. In books from the 18th and 19th centuries, it is common to find bookplates decorated with the owner's family crest. Bookplates often include the text "Ex Libris," Latin for "from the library of. . . ."

From the earliest days of manuscript books up to the present day, readers, and not necessarily book owners, have written in books. This habit is something with which most readers of *A Brief History of the Book* can personally identify. Perhaps, as you have been reading your copy of this book, you have been underlining passages that you have deemed important (the author hopes there are at least a few). Perhaps you have been placing checkmarks in the margins to note sections that you might want to review later. If you have, you are engaging in a long tradition of readers interacting with books. A dramatic example of relatively early reader annotation is the famous

Lindisfarne Gospels produced in the late 17th century in Northumbria, England, on the island of Lindisfarne.[28] Known for its beautiful and elaborate decorations, the text is the Latin translation of the four Gospels. Written above the Latin text is an Old English translation written nearly 300 years later. This is the oldest surviving English translation of the Gospels. The *Lindisfarne Gospels* is preserved in the British Library (see https://www.bl .uk/collection-items/lindisfarne-gospels).

From the medieval period through to the modern age, readers note important passages of text using various systems. Some might mark "NB" in the margins for the Latin "*nota bene*" or "note well." Some might draw a hand pointing to the printed text. This mark is called a manicule (or some libraries have cataloged them as "fists"). Figure 3-20 is an example of a manicule from a book printed c. 1470 that reports on the recent Turkish invasion of the island of Eubeoa. An early reader clearly wanted to note a passage of text and drew a detailed manicule, complete with fingernails. Readers might use manuscript annotations to express their own reactions and opinions on the text. They might even mark up their books for some other use, such as a minister preparing someone else's sermon for delivery, or an actor or director marking up the text of a play.[29] Any manuscript annotation serves as evidence of how readers might have responded to or used their books.

Readers also leave behind other physical evidence. Wear and tear and debris in the gutter might indicate more heavily used pages of the book. Dog-eared corners, pins, or bookmarks might note important pages. Some reader interaction with books might not actually concern the texts. Empty spaces in books might be an inviting canvas for doodles or, as is often the case in family Bibles, a site for recording genealogical information. The weight of a book might be ideal for pressing flowers and leaves. Books have been an important part of human lives for centuries and have diverse functions. Often, if we study them closely, we can learn more about the lives that books have led.

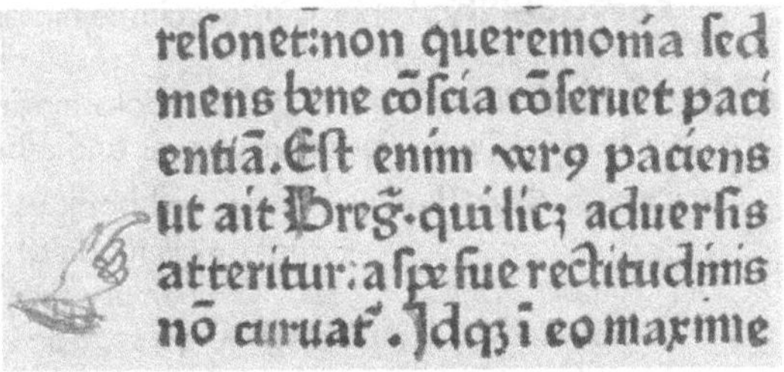

Figure 3-20   A manicule drawn in Rodericus Zamorensis, *Epistola de expugnatione Nigropontis* (Cologne: Ulrich Zel, c. 1470–71). RIT Cary Graphic Arts Collection. Photograph by Jordan Funk.

MODERN ADS FOR EARLY TECHNOLOGIES

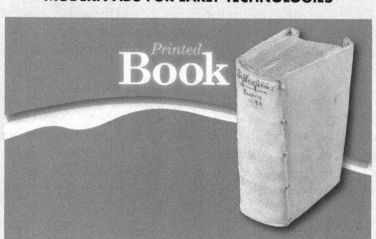

Figure 3-21   Printed Book. Designed by Amelia Fontanel.

Printed Book

Memory: As with its predecessor the manuscript book, the printed book varied in physical sizes and could expand into innumerable additional volumes.

Readable/writable: While there are examples of books being printed on parchment, the chief medium was initially laid paper made from linen pulp and more recently paper made from wood pulp. While paper is sturdy, it does not allow for the easy erasure of printed ink.

Recyclability: Paper is a recyclable material. Early linen paper might be durable enough to find new uses, including bookbinding material or pie-plate liners.[57] Today, books made from paper pulp are recycled into new wood-pulp paper and other paper-based products.

Durability: The life of a printed book usually depends more on how it is cared for than what it was made of. That said, books printed on linen paper in the mid-15th century survive today in excellent condition and should continue to do so, barring any negative interactions with natural elements such as water and fire, or irresponsible or malignant humans. Wood-pulp paper is less durable and might become brittle over time.

Security: The binding options available for medieval manuscript books continued into the age of printed books. This might range from a book with no binding or a simple paper wrapper, to a sturdy leather binding, to an elaborate artists' binding.

Access: As with the manuscript book and all codices, the printed book offers its users random access. By turning to any page, the reader can access any part of the book almost instantly.

Cost: $–$$$$. The cost of printed books can vary a great deal. Mass-produced paperback books can be acquired very inexpensively, whereas fine press or artists' books might be quite expensive.

HORNBOOK: ANOTHER EARLY HANDHELD

Figure 3-22 An English hornbook c. 1600. RIT Cary Graphic Arts Collection.

During the 16th and 17th centuries, books took on other interesting, handheld formats. One of the most well-known educational tools was the hornbook. Hornbooks were handhelds used in England, and later in America, for teaching children to read. Figure 3-22 shows an example from the Cary Collection dating back to England in the late 16th or early 17th century. The date and place of origin of this hornbook is evidenced by its binding style—calfskin with brass bosses stamped with the Tudor Rose. The wood is paddle-shaped so it can be held by the tutor in front of the child. As with this example, the text of hornbooks usually consisted of the alphabet and the "Our Father" prayer. Hornbooks get their name from the thin layer of animal horn that is used to cover and protect the printed sheet. Animal horn was the original Gorilla Glass.

THE BOOK IN THE 19TH CENTURY: INDUSTRIALIZING PRINTING

The wooden common hand press remained the main technology used for printing books in Europe and America from its introduction by Gutenberg in the 1450s until about 1800. Generally, the technology of the printing press and movable metal type did not change dramatically over the course of its first 350 years.[30] Through the early 19th century, however, technological advances began to change printing and the making of books.

The first major advancement in printing was the move from the wooden press to the iron press. The first successful iron platen press was developed in England by Charles Stanhope, 3rd Earl Stanhope (1753–1816), beginning in about 1800, figure 3-23. This invention was made possible by advancements in metal casting.[31] Stanhope's design was quite similar to the wooden press, except that, most significantly, he reinforced the screw of the wooden press with a system of compound levers. Following Stanhope's, two of the most successful iron presses were the Columbian press produced in 1816 by George E. Clymer (1754–1834) of Philadelphia (who soon thereafter moved his company to England) and the Albion iron hand press developed in England. Iron presses were not only more durable than wooden ones, but their iron platens were larger than their wooden predecessors. Large, flat, iron platens created a sharper, more consistent impression. What's more, the larger platen meant that the press operator need pull only one impression for every sheet rather than the two pulls needed for each sheet when using a wooden press. By the 1820s, most printers in Europe had iron presses. American printers would make the same transition shortly thereafter, in particular with the popularity of the relatively lightweight and reliable Washington iron press.[32]

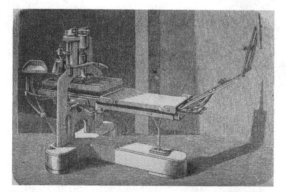

Figure 3-23   Stanhope Press. Caleb Stower, *The Printer's Grammar; or, Introduction to the Art of Printing* (London: B. Crosby and Co., 1808), frontispiece. RIT Cary Graphic Arts Collection.

PAPER

The production of paper also changed significantly due to technological advances. In the middle of the 18th century, the production of handmade paper shifted from laid paper, as described earlier in this chapter, to wove paper. The process of making wove paper was similar to that of laid paper, but the wires of mold were woven tightly together, rather than spaced out. As Dard Hunter describes, "The 'wove' covering was made of fine brass screening and received its name from being woven on a loom in about the same manner as cloth. It left in the paper an indistinct impression resembling a fabric."[33] As a result, wove paper has no chain lines when examined with a light pad. The invention of wove paper is often traced back to the British paper mill of James Whatman (1702–1759). The first known book to use wove paper appears to be an edition of Virgil, *Publii Virgilii Maronis Bucolica, Georgica, et Aeneis* printed by John Baskerville (1706–1775) in Birmingham in 1757.[34] For helpful illustrations of laid and wove paper and the molds that create them, visit this page from the American Bookbinders Museum in San Francisco, California: https://bookbinders museum.org/a-brief-history-of-wove-paper.

Prior to the 19th century, paper was made chiefly of linen rags, after which new substrates were being investigated. Wood pulp paper was being advanced in about 1800, as evidenced by a book printed in that year, with a second edition in 1801, by Matthias Koops (fl. 1789–1805), titled *Historical Account of the Substances Which Have Been Used to Describe Events, and to Convey Ideas, from the Earliest Date to the Invention of Paper*. Koops was looking for new substances from which to make paper. Demonstrating his findings, the majority of his book was printed on paper made from what may seem an unusual material—hay. Unsurprisingly, this choice gives the paper a yellowish hue. His book's appendix, however, was printed on a different substance—wood pulp paper. He writes:

> As an appendix to this little tract, I think it proper to submit a few more remarks on the National Importance of discovering materials which can be converted into Paper, and grow sufficiently abundant in Great Britain, without the necessity of importing them from foreign countries. The following lines are printed upon Paper made from Wood alone. . . .[35]

Koops established a paper mill in 1801 that failed the next year. The successful production and adoption of wood pulp paper would have to wait until the middle of the 19th century. American books, for example, were still printed on rag paper until 1849. Thereafter, wood pulp paper slowly took over the market to the extent that "by the last thirty years of the century the transition was completed, nearly all book papers being made of mixtures of rag, straw, mechanical wood, and chemical wood in varying proportions."[36]

Meanwhile, the production of paper became mechanized. In 1801 in England, Henry Fourdrinier (1766–1854) and his brother Sealy Fourdrinier (1773–1847) backed the development of a mechanical process for making paper invented by Nicolas-Louis Robert (1761–1828). Liquid pulp from a vat was poured onto a wire belt. As the pulp traveled along the belt, the water drained from it. Felt rollers pressed the pulp dry and even. Eventually, the dried paper sheet was rolled up into a continuous web of paper.[37] Such large rolls of paper were not yet helpful for printers producing books on hand presses, since the paper would have to be cut into sheets, but would soon be advantageous for printers of newspapers using mechanized presses.[38]

MECHANIZED PRINTING PRESSES

The first attempts at mechanizing printing presses used steam power to move the traditional platens of hand presses. But the answer lay not in repurposing hand presses in this way, but rather in the reworking of a different style of platen. Inspired by the cylinder platens used when printing copperplate engravings, an Englishman named William Nicholson (1753–1815) began working in the 1790s with a cylindrical platen that would roll over the inked printing type and paper. Thus the impression was made with consistent pressure as the cylinder rolled over the type. He patented this machine in 1790, but it was never built.[39]

The first successful cylinder press was developed by a German inventor named Friedrich Koenig (1774–1833), who was living in England. In 1814, a steam-powered cylinder printing press produced by Koenig was installed in *The Times* (of London). The first issue of *The Times* to be printed on his press appeared on November 29, 1814.[40] On that day, the paper proudly announced:

Our Journal of this day presents to the public the practical result of the greatest improvement connected with printing, since the discovery of the art itself. The reader of this paragraph now holds in his hand, one of the many thousand impressions of *The Times* newspaper, which were taken off last night by a mechanical apparatus. A system of machinery almost organic has been devised and arranged, which, while it relieves the human frame of its most laborious efforts in printing, far exceeds all human powers in rapidity and dispatch. That the magnitude of the invention may be justly appreciated by its effects, we shall inform the public, that after the letters are placed by the compositors, and enclosed in what is called the form, little more remains for man to do, than to attend upon, and watch this unconscious agent in its operations. The machine is then merely supplied with paper: itself places the form, inks it, adjusts the paper to the form newly inked, stamps the sheet, and gives it forth to the hands of the attendant, at the same time withdrawing the form for a fresh coat of ink, which itself again distributes, to meet the ensuing sheet now advancing for impression; and the whole of these complicated acts is performed with such a velocity and simultaneousness of movement, that no less than eleven hundred sheets are impressed in one hour.[41]

Indeed, as Banham notes, Koenig's machine's 1,100 sheets an hour more than tripled "the 300 sheets an hour on an iron hand press."[42] Two years later, Koenig improved the design so that it would print the front and back of the sheet off of two formes of type at the same time.

Production was very high, but the printing quality was not—though it was well-suited to the production of newspapers, which were printed daily and were not intended to last. Some printers of books wanted higher printing quality and continued to use hand presses. Beginning in the 1830s, most English printers were switching over to powered platen presses and later to higher-quality cylinder presses. American printers followed suit toward the middle of the century. In this way, even smaller printing houses had become printing factories.[43]

ADVANCES IN TYPESETTING

In the 19th century, printing innovations extended into methods for setting type. There were several advances, but the ones that had the most profound effects were the use of stereotype plates, and the invention of the Linotype machine by Ottmar Mergenthaler and the Monotype machine by Tolbert Lanston.

Stereotypes

Creating a stereotype, or cliché, was a method that allowed a printer to make printing plates that could be used repeatedly. Typical printing-house practice did not allow for "standing type," that is, keeping type standing in formes waiting for later use. Printers did not have infinite founts of type, and they usually worked on concurrent projects and moved from job to job. Thus, once a forme was printed, the type was redistributed into its cases and new formes were typeset. Stereotyping created a way for printers to have reusable plates for printing their most popular books. Once the compositor had set a forme, papier mâché was beaten over the type creating a mold of the pages in the forme. Molten lead was then poured into this negative mold or "flong," casting a plate that, when fastened to a block and made type-high, could be used on a press.[44] These plates would be kept and used whenever particular books needed to be reprinted—books such as school primers and Bibles were perfect candidates for creating stereotype plates. The technology of making stereotype plates dates back to the 18th century, but was advanced and popularized in the 19th century. This technology later lent itself well to the production of curved printing plates that permitted the use of rotary presses. For example, *The Times* of London again pushed printing technology forward in the 1860s when they installed a rotary printing that could print "10,000 copies of complete newspapers in an hour."[45]

Linotype and Monotype

Created in Baltimore in 1886 by a German immigrant, Ottmar Mergenthaler (1854–1899), the Linotype typesetting machine dramatically increased the rate of type composition by mechanizing the process of typesetting. Rather than having to set individual pieces of type by hand, the Linotype machine allowed typesetters to produce an entire line of type (thus, Linotype) mechanically by entering the text via a keyboard. As the typesetter typed, corresponding brass matrices (mats) for the letters were arranged in a line, along with spacebands used to separate the words. Type metal, kept in a molten state in the machine, was then injected into the matrices, producing one complete line of type.[46] Figure 3-24 is row of set Linotype matrices separated by space bands. To the right is a single Linotype matrix. Below them a cast line of type or "slug." After casting, the lines of type were transferred into a galley, just as typesetters had done before with lines of type set in a composing stick. However, with Linotype slugs, all the compositor had to do was stack the lines.[47]

The Monotype, patented in 1887 and made commercially available in 1897 by Tolbert Lanston (1844–1913), worked in a similar, though more complicated, fashion.[48] The system consisted of two different machines. A keyboard was used to input text that was communicated via coded paper tape to a caster, as described in a contemporary account printed in the *Inland Printer Journal* in 1893:

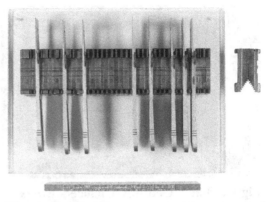

Figure 3-24 Linotype matrices separated by spacebands, with a single matrix and a cast line of type. RIT Cary Graphic Arts Collection.

> A machine little known to the craft at large, but which is apt to create a furor someday, is the Lanston monotype, which casts separate type of the usual commercial form, at the same time setting them in justified lines, the operation being controlled by strips of paper containing small round holes which have previously been punched by another machine or keyboard.[49]

The Monotype's output differed from that of Linotype. Rather than producing one single connected line of type, Monotype cast a complete ready-to-print galley of individual pieces of type. This made for easier typographic corrections. As Gaskell notes, this aspect of the Monotype system made it quite successful in Europe, where "book printers were attracted by the fact that its individual types could be handled and printed in the same way as hand-set type."[50]

All of these 19th-century advancements, iron and steam-powered presses, wood pulp paper, and mechanized composing machines led to the unprecedented production of books and other reading material.

FINE PRESS BOOKS

While industrialized book production led to wider access to books, the quality of printing tended to suffer as a result. Toward the end of the 19th century, some printers were inspired to reclaim their heritage and put traditional craftsmanship back into the art of book production. This

Figure 3-25 Geoffrey Chaucer, *Works of Geoffrey Chaucer* (Hammersmith, Middlesex: Kelmscott Press, 1896). RIT Cary Graphic Arts Collection. Photograph by Shannon Taggart.

revival of the art of the book was a part of the greater Arts and Crafts movement that emerged in Great Britain and traveled overseas to the United States. English artists such as William Morris (1834–1896) of the Kelmscott Press and T. J. Cobden-Sanderson (1840–1922) of the Doves Press, and the American Elbert Hubbard (1856–1915) of the Roycroft Press in the United States began to make beautiful books using handmade paper printed on hand presses with handsomely designed type and illustrations, and bound in fine bindings. William Morris's edition of *The Works of Geoffrey Chaucer* (Hammersmith, Middlesex: Kelmscott Press, 1896) is often cited as the most dramatic book of this period, as shown in figure 3-25. Books such as *The Kelmscott Chaucer,* as it is more informally called, inspired generations of fine press printers and book artists, who continue to advance the art of the book and push the boundaries of what books can be.

TYPEWRITERS

Typewriters were invented in the 19th century and continued to be an important writing technology through the late 20th century. Although hardly used today, aspects of the typewriter have influenced the digital world. Many different typewriters or "writing machines" were invented in the 19th century. For example, the Cary Graphic Arts Collection holds a patent report from 1848 that contains an early patent for a writing machine invented by Charles Thurber (1803–1886). The patent notes:

A very elaborate machine for writing has been patented, evidently the fruits of deep study; and, in view of the complexity of results produced by this contrivance, the construction is exceedingly simple, as well as its operation. The object of the invention is to furnish to those who are unable to write, the means of writing, by sitting before a set of keys, the mere touching of which immediately causes the corresponding letter to be written upon a sheet of paper.[51]

It is very interesting that the purpose of the writing machine was to help those who cannot write, that is, those who cannot write by hand. Today we might think that typewriters were invented primarily to speed up written production or facilitate "printing" at home or in a business environment. But, in the case of this patent, it appears to be more about the ability to record information by means of keystrokes rather than writing out a text by hand.

The first commercial typewriter to hit the market was produced in 1874 by the E. Remington & Sons Arms Company.[52] The 19th-century invention of keyboards for inputting text would become a crucial feature in the late 20th century in the invention of personal computers, word processors, tablet computers, PDAs, and smartphones. In this case, it is the QWERTY keyboard that had the most impact in the United States. Patented in 1878 by the American printer Christopher Latham Sholes (1819–1890), the QWERTY keyboard is the layout that we usually find on our devices, figure 3-26. Why did Sholes arrange the keys in an unfamiliar manner? As Torbjörn Lundmark notes, the keys were laid out in this fashion to "move common letter-pairs away from each other" in order to slow down the typist, so that speed of his or her typing would not cause the bars of the typewriter to get stuck.[53] One peculiar aspect of the QWERTY layout is the hidden word embedded in the keyboard's top line. Indeed, if you look carefully, you will notice that the letters contained in the top line of the QWERTY keyboard can be rearranged to spell the word "typewriter."[54] This has led to speculation that this was intended for salesmen to dazzle customers by typing "typewriter" with great speed.

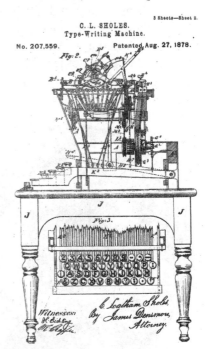

Figure 3-26 The 1878 patent for Christopher Latham Sholes "Type-Writing Machine" with QWERTY keyboard. US Patent 207,559.

QWERTY is just one style of keyboard—there were and continue to be many different layouts. Even Sholes himself introduced a new keyboard layout shortly before his death. Yet QWERTY was picked up by Remington for its typewriters, and the layout stuck. For the most part, at least in the United States, the QWERTY has endured, even finding its way onto the tablets and smartphones we use daily. It is perhaps more than a little strange that we still use QWERTY, a keyboard system designed in the 19th century, to input our digital information.

PHOTOTYPESETTING

Hot metal typesetting technologies such as Linotype and Monotype continued through most of the 20th century. In the 1940s and 1950s, a new system of setting type through photographic means brought the typesetting technology from lead to light.[55] In 1946, French inventors Louis Marius Moyroud (1914–2010) and Rene Alphonse Higonnet (1902–1983) developed a machine through which inputting text using a keyboard caused a strobe light to shine through a matrix of negative letters, numbers, and other characters, thereby exposing them on photographic film. In this way, text was set photographically without setting any metal type. The photographic layout was then used to create a printing plate. Higonnet and Moyroud's systems were called Lumitype and Photon. Figure 3-27 is an example a matrix, or disc containing negative characters that would rotate within the phototypesetting machine. It is from the late 1970s by a company called Varityper. The font on this disk is Lubalin Graph.

Figure 3-27   A Varityper phototypesetting matrix. RIT Cary Graphic Arts Collection.

The very first book typeset using phototypesetting technology, Albro

Gaul's *The Wonderful World of Insects*, was published in 1953. A note at the end of the book explains its historical importance:

> *The Wonderful World of Insects* derives added significance from the manner in which it was composed. It is the first volume composed with the revolutionary Higonnet-Moyroud photographic type-composing machine. Absolutely no type, in the conventional sense, was used in the preparation of this book.[56]

Although, today, phototypesetting is not a well-known innovation outside of those familiar with printing history, at the time it was hailed as an invention as revolutionary as Gutenberg's printing press. This was not hyperbolic. Phototypesetting did change printing technology in a most profound way. Yet, on the time line of the history of the book, its relatively brief life span of several decades causes the technology to be underappreciated. Phototypesetting was the technology that bridged the gap between making books printed with metal type and making books with digital technology.

FURTHER READING

Banham, Rob. "The Industrialization of the Book, 1800–1970." In *Companion to the History of the Book*, edited by Simon Eliot and Jonathan Rose, 273–290. Malden, MA: Blackwell, 2007.

British Library. *Treasures in Full: Gutenberg Bible.* https://www.bl.uk/treasures/gutenberg/homepage.html.

Gaskell, Philip. *A New Introduction to Bibliography.* New York; Oxford: Oxford University Press, 1972.

Twyman, Michael. *The British Library Guide to Printing: History and Techniques.* Toronto: University of Toronto Press, 1998.

ACTIVITIES

Activity 3: Setting and Proofing Type

Objectives

Readers will get a sense of the work of a compositor by pulling type from a type case and setting it into a composing stick. The most effective way to understand printing on a hand press is to actively do it—and, preferably in a manner that shows the process from typesetting through to printing. If at all possible, reach out to a nearby book arts center, museum, or library that has a printing press, or a local printer. I think you will find that people involved with printing are usually quite happy to share their knowledge and experience with you.

If access to a printing press is not a possibility, then there are creative ways to engage with foundational aspects of the printing process. In this activity, readers will learn how founts of printing type are housed in type cases, the lay (organization) of the case, and how a compositor sets type in a composing stick. Most of the material listed below can be purchased used on Ebay and Amazon.

Supplies

- Diagram of layout of California job case (see figure 3-6). Printable images of the California job case are easily found online.
- California job case (type case).
- Font of printing type, distributed into the California job case using the layout as your guide. A point size of 12 or 14 is recommended. Used fonts of type are available on Ebay. Newly cast type can be purchased on sites like Skyline Type Foundry (https://skylinetype .com).
- Leading (thin horizontal spacing material made of lead) of various sizes. 10- to 24-pica lengths should cover the length of most lines.
- 3M or 4M quads, and en and em quads in the same point size (or height) as your type.
- A variety of copper and brass thins spacers (optional, but helpful).
- Several composing sticks.
- Thin string or page-cord for tying type.
- Large stamp pad. 5 × 7 inches is a good size.
- Rubber brayer (optional).
- Baby wipes.

Instructions

Setting Type

1. Choose a short passage of text.
2. If working with a group, assign a line of text to each participant.

3. Set the composing sticks to a pica length that will accommodate the longest line of text.

4. Insert a slug of leading of the same pica length that the stick is set to.

5. Begin to set your text. Pull type from the case, using the California job case layout as your guide. Holding the composing stick in your left hand, start in the lower left corner of the stick, and set each letter upside down from left to right. Use your thumb to guide and hold the type. If you are setting type properly, the nicks or grooves of the type will line up along the belly or side of type facing you.

6. Set a 3M quad between each word. If the text does not fill the entire line and space remains, fill the empty space using en and em quads (as well as 3M and 4M quads). Try to make each line as snug as possible. Inserting thin copper and brass spacers is helpful in creating a snug line.

7. Once you have finished your first line, begin setting the next line below it. You may wish to insert another line of leading, but it is not necessary.

8. Continue to set your text, letter by letter, word by word, and line by line.

9. When the passage is set, or the stick is full, insert another line of leading over the last line set.

Proofing the Text

At this point, the text is usually transferred into a galley tray to be proofed. For this exercise, we will proof the text using pressure printing while the type is still in the composing stick.

1. Secure the type by tying it up. Wrap string tightly five times around the lines of type and leading. Take the loose end of the string and tuck it behind the layers of string.

2. Ink the type by carefully pressing the large ink pad down onto the top of the type.

3. Place a blank sheet of paper on top of the inked type. Make an impression using pressure printing. This can be done by pressing down with your hand or rolling a rubber brayer over the paper.

4. Carefully check your print to see if you have set your text properly. The printed impression likely will not be crisp, but it should be legible.

Cleaning and Distributing the Type

1. Use baby wipes to wipe the remaining ink off the type.
2. Carefully distribute the type back into the case.

Helpful Resources

*   https://www.paekakarikipress.com/?content=content/southward/TyingUpPages.html
*   https://letterpresscommons.com/setting-type-by-hand
*   https://www.youtube.com/watch?v=AHrLIVeH1KM

Activity 4: Writing a History of a Book

Objectives

Use your powers of deduction and your burgeoning knowledge of book history to examine a book for evidence of its history.

Supplies

*   A book or books with evidence of previous readers and owners.

Write a history of the book that you have chosen to study. Examine in detail the book's physical makeup, text, production history, and provenance. Here is an outline of aspects to consider.

Instructions

Examining a Book

1. Author and title
2. Date of publication
3. Genre and nature of the text(s)
4. Format of the book
5. Style of bookbinding and any edge decoration
6. Condition of the bookbinding and the pages throughout (a page-by-page examination is encouraged)

Evidence to Look For

1. Ownership marks
    a. Ownership signatures, bookplates
    b. Library stamps, pencil inscription such as call numbers

2. Notes regarding the sale
    a. An earlier price might be indicated by the Latin word "pretium"
    b. Later booksellers often pencil in the price in the upper corner of a front endpaper
    c. Sometimes book owners cut out the book's description from the bookseller's or auction catalog and past the description on one of the front endpapers
3. Evidence of use
    a. Manuscript annotations (check every page!)
    b. Significant wear and tear
    c. Dog-eared corners, bookmarks, and other ways of marking pages
    d. Objects left in books such as flowers

Describe your book as a physical artifact. What is its format (folio, quarto, octavo, etc.)? How, when, and by whom was it bound? Describe any other important physical features.

Describe the book's text(s). Who is the author(s) of your text? What is the text and its history? Is there more than one text? Had the text(s) been printed before, and was it reprinted thereafter? Who was the audience for the text? Is there any preliminary matter, and what is its purpose?

Describe the production of your book. Who is the printer(s)/publisher(s)? When and where was it published? Where was it sold? Can you identify the paper used? What sort of type is used? Is your book illustrated? If so, how and by whom? Were the illustrations commissioned for this book, or were they reused?

Describe the provenance of your book? Can you trace the book's history using evidence found in the book? Create a time line. At the top of the page, write the book's place of publication. At the bottom of the page, write the book's current home. Can you fill in the time line between? Who owned your book over the centuries? How did your book end up in its current location? Is there any evidence suggesting how readers interacted with the book?

NOTES

1. David J. Marcou, "Korea the Cradle of Movable Metal Type," *Korean Culture* 13.1 (1992): 4; Pow-key Sohn, "Early Korean Printing," *Journal of the American Oriental Society* 79.2 (1959): 98.

2. Quoted from Song Hyon, "Yongjae ch'onghwa," *Taedong yasung* (Seoul, 1909), 1, 158; Sohn, "Early Korean Printing," 99.

3. Ibid., 99.

4. Kornicki, Peter, "Japan, Korea, and Vietnam," 119.

5. Ch'on Hye-Bong, "Pulcho Chikchi Simch'e Yojol," *Korean Journal* 3 (1963): 12. In this article, Hye-Bong provides a detailed bibliographic description of *Chikchi Simch'e yojol*.

6. For a brief, but detailed, overview see Eric Marshall White, *Editio princeps: A History of the Gutenberg Bible* (London; Turnhout: Harvey Miller Publishers, 2017): 21–39.

7. White, 25.

8. Frédéric Barbier, *Gutenberg's Europe: The Book and the Invention of Western Modernity* (Cambridge, UK; Malden, MA, USA: Polity, 2017), 114–115.

9. Marcou, 7.

10. White, 42–45; https://www.bl.uk/treasures/gutenberg/prtgutdonatus .html.

11. A contemporary notice of the printing of the Gutenberg Bible survives in a letter from March 12, 1455, and mentions the print run at both 158 and 180 copies (White 23). For an informative overview of the history of the Gutenberg Bible, see https://www.bl.uk/treasures/gutenberg/home page.html.

12. See White, 47 and especially his census of Gutenberg Bible, 307–333.

13. Benjamin Franklin, *The Autobiography of Benjamin Franklin*, ed. Leonard W. Labaree (New Haven, CT: Yale University Press, 1964), 119.

14. Special thanks to the student team: Seth Gottlieb, Daniel Krull, Ferris Nicolais, Veronica Hebbard, and Randall Paulhamus. To read an account of the creation of the "Uncommon" Press, see https://printinghistory.org /author/sgottlieb.

15. Robert A. Thom, *Benjamin Franklin*, oil on canvas, 32 × 24 inches, Kimberly Clark Graphic Communications through the Ages Series, ca. 1960.

16. Philip Gaskell, *A New Introduction to Bibliography* (New York; Oxford: Oxford University Press, 1972), 139.

17. Eric White of the Bridwell Library has gathered data to create "A Census of Print Runs for Fifteenth-Century Books." White's research presents a more quantitative approach to understanding print runs in the incunabula period. See "Researching Print Runs" for an overview and census at https://www.cerl.org/resources/links_to_other_resources/bibliographical _data.

18. Gaskell, 161.

19. Raymond Clemens and Timothy Graham, *Introduction to Manuscript Studies* (Ithaca, NY: Cornell University Press, 2007), 3.

20. Martin Davies, *Aldus Manutius: Printer and Publisher of Renaissance Venice* (Tempe, AZ: Arizona Center for Medieval and Renaissance Studies, 1999), 42.

21. Eloise Pafort, "Notes on the Wynkyn De Worde Editions of the 'Boke of St. Albans' and Its Separates." *Studies in Bibliography* 5 (1952): 43–52. See also H. S. Bennett, *English Books & Readers 1603–1640; Being a Study in the History of the Book Trade in the Reigns of James I and Charles I* (Cambridge [England]: University Press, 1969), 24.

22. For instances where folios use less paper than smaller formats, see Steven K. Galbraith, "English Literary Folios 1593–1623," *Tudor Books and Readers Materiality and the Construction of Meaning,* ed. John N. King (Cambridge: Cambridge University Press, 2010), 46–67.

23. http://www.perseus.tufts.edu/hopper/morph?l=incunabula&la=la# lexicon.

24. Margaret M. Smith, *The Title-Page, Its Early Development, 1460–1510* (Castle, DE: Oak Knoll Press, 2000), 22.

25. Ibid., 75–89.

26. Ibid., 22.

27. See Henry Petroski, *The Book on the Bookshelf* (New York: Alfred A. Knopf: Distributed by Random House, 1999), 150; Graham Pollard, *Changes in the Style of Bookbinding, 1550–1830* (London; New York: Oxford University Press, 1956), 92–93; and Steven K. Galbraith, *Edges of Books* (Rochester, NY: Cary Graphic Arts Press, 2012).

28. Backhouse, J. (2003). Lindisfarne Gospels. *Grove Art Online.* https://www.oxfordartonline.com/groveart/view/10.1093/gao/9781884446054.001.0001/oao-9781884446054-e-7000051172 (accessed November 9, 2019).

29. See Steven K. Galbraith, "Latimer Revised and Reprised: Editing *Frutefull Sermons* for Pulpit Delivery," *Reformation* 11 (2006): 29–46.

30. Though I should say that the student engineers that worked on RIT's "Uncommon Press" found subtle but interesting changes in the design of the wooden common press. For example, see https://printinghistory.org/uncommon-reconstruction.

31. James Moran, *Printing Presses; History and Development from the Fifteenth Century to Modern Times* (Berkeley, CA: University of California Press, 1973), 49.

32. Gaskell, 198.

33. Dard Hunter, *Papermaking: The History and Technique of an Ancient Craft* (New York: Dover Publications, 1978), 127.

34. J. N. Balston, *The Whatmans and Wove Paper: Its Invention and Development in the West* (West Farleigh, Kent: John Balston, 1998), xxxiv; Hunter, 125.

35. Matthias Koops, *Historical Account of the Substances Which Have Been Used to Describe Events, and to Convey Ideas, from the Earliest Date to the Invention of Paper* (London: Printed by Jacques and Co., 1801), 85.

36. Gaskell, 222.

37. Hunter, 346; Gaskell, 217.

38. Hunter, 348.

39. Gaskell, 251.

40. Michael Twyman, *The British Library Guide to Printing: History and Techniques* (Toronto: University of Toronto Press, 1998), 70.

41. *The Times*, Tuesday, November 29, 1814, Issue 9378, p. 3.

42. Rob Banham, "The Industrialization of the Book, 1800–1970," in *Companion to the History of the Book,* ed. Simon Eliot and Jonathan Rose (Malden, MA: Blackwell, 2007), 276. Gaskell presents similar numbers ". . . capable in practice of turning out 900 perfected double-demy sheets per hour. This may be compared with the maximum output of 150 such sheets per hour which might just be reached, with much effort, by a large iron hand-press" (252).

43. Gaskell, 253–254.

44. Banham, 279.

45. Twyman, 71.

46. Frank J. Romano, *History of the Linotype Company* (Rochester, NY: RIT Press, 2014), 75.

47. For an illustrated history of "Mergenthaler's Linotype Machines, 1883–1972," see Romano, 75–114.

48. *The Lanston Monotype: Two Articles on the Lanston Monotype Machine Reprinted from the Pages of the Inland Printer* (Rochester, NY: Press of the Good Mountain, 1970), 8–9.

49. Ibid., 11.

50. Gaskell, 281.

51. United States, Patent Office, *Annual Report of the Commissioner of Patents: Report of the Commissioner of Patents, for the Year 1845* (Washington: Ritchie & Heiss, print, 1846), 32–33.

52. Torbjörn Lundmark, *Quirky Qwerty: The Story of the Keyboard @ Your Fingertips* (UNSW, Sydney, NSW: UNSW Press, 2002), 10

53. Ibid., 17. See also Paul A. David, "Clio and the Economics of QWERTY," *The American Economic Review* 75.2 (1985): 333.

54. Lundmark, 19.

55. "From Lead to Light" is the translation of the title of a major book on phototypesetting, Alan Marshall, *Du plomb à la lumière. La Lumitype-Photon et la naissances des industries graphiques modernes* (Paris: Éditions de la Maison des sciences de l'homme, 2003).

56. Albro Tilton Gaul, *The Wonderful World of Insects* (New York: Rinehart, 1953), 291.

57. For the latter, see various accounts of John Warburton and his cook, Betsy Baker.

FOUR

Digital Books

A BRIEF AND QUIRKY HISTORY OF MODERN TABLETS

When one visualizes a time line of the history of the book, an obvious theme that emerges is the astounding increase in the speed of technological change moving from the ancient world to the present. At the very beginning of the time line are cuneiform tablets, a technology that appeared around 3200 BCE and was in use into the first century CE. Papyrus rolls appeared in approximately 3000 BCE and were in use until the early centuries in the first millennium CE. This is roughly the same total amount of time as cuneiform was in use. Parchment and paper rolls continue to be used today by some cultures around the world. The codex came into its own in around the fourth century in manuscript form, and then in the mid-15th century in print. All in all, the codex is about 2,000 years old and still a part of everyday life in most parts of the world. The evolution of the codex is remarkable. It begins with about 1,500 years of producing books by hand, to roughly 450 years of printing primarily with a hand press, to about 200 years of manufacturing books with mechanical machines.

The time line of the history of the book culminates for now at the early 21st century with the development of digital reading devices. If the arrival of personal computers dates to the mid-1970s, then the age of reading digitally spans a comparatively brief history of 45 years. If the focus is on just handheld personal digital assistants, tablet computers, and e-readers, then the time frame is a mere 25 brief years. Yet the technological changes across this short period have been extraordinary. This is the nature of the time line of the history of the book. If the ancient world was measured in millennia, and the Middle Ages and European Renaissance in centuries, then the late 20th and early 21st centuries are measured in years, months, and even days. This essentially means that the most recent developments in the book are moving targets. Not only can it be a challenge to identify what contemporary media to study, it is even more of a challenge to identify or predict future trends. The *future* of reading and writing, and the circulation of text and image, is a rapidly evolving *present* in which most users are actively participating—in real time.

This rapid speed of change also renders certain technologies obsolete at a much faster pace. This means that a technology that might have been a part of our daily lives at one point or another might simultaneously feel both familiar and foreign. Clearly, such a technology is not as foreign, as say an ancient Egyptian roll, but technologies from even a decade or two ago can feel somehow unfamiliar because so much has changed so intensely in such a short period of time. Take, for example, the cordless telephone. For many people, the only time you might see a corldless phone is on a television screen while watching reruns of sitcoms from the 1990s. These older phones are immediately notable for their large size, and further notable for the fact that you rarely see them in everyday life. In most offices, you will find traditional landline phones, but cordless phones are once-popular communication devices that are going the way of the dodo.

Perhaps in some ways, some of the more recently obsolete objects are stranger to us than, for example, a cuneiform tablet. When readers handle a clay tablet for the first time, they instinctively hold it properly in their hands and begin to try to "read" it. They likely will not know the language, but they know the format—the handheld. They are familiar with holding similar-sized devices in their hands about 16 inches or so from their eyes—a similar comfortable distance, more or less, between the eyes and the text on the device when reading or writing. This gesture seems a natural human act or at least has evolved into one. In addition to being about the same distance and position used with modern tablets, it is an action very near to our handling of printed books—a behavior that begins at least with ancient wax tablets. When readers first handle a wax tablet, they immediately and naturally begin to operate it, opening it as if it were a printed book or a laptop. This is a well-known format—the codex. Although an ancient medium, wax tablets are direct ancestors of the handheld reading and writing technologies that we use each day. Rolls or scrolls are a somewhat different medium. They are a technology that continues in some cultures in its basic form, while enduring more pervasively as an action. To scroll—as a verb—is an ancient idea applied to the use of modern digital devices. While many readers never use scrolls, they regularly scroll through pages on their smartphones and on websites.

When modern readers hold a tablet computer, flip through a printed book, or scroll through digital pages on a smartphone, they are engaging with the past *and* present simultaneously. This should come as no surprise. When we study the history of the book, we often see history repeating itself.

THE KINDLE: A BRIEF HISTORY OF THE BOOK IN ONE DEVICE

The Amazon Kindle debuted to great enthusiasm in 2007, selling out in a matter of hours.[1] The Kindle shown in figure 4-1 was not the first e-reader. Fairly successful models had appeared about a decade earlier, but it became the device that put e-book readers firmly on the map. Because of this, in the long history of tablets and books more generally, the Kindle is a milestone. What's more, in the most interesting ways, the Kindle manifests, in its physical form, the history presented in the first three chapters of *A Brief History of the Book*. In fact, this book could have begun with the 2007 Kindle and rewound back through the history of the book—tablet to tablet, cuneiform to Kindle.

Amazon founder and CEO Jeff Bezos (1964–) very well understood that his new device was the latest addition to the long evolution of the book. He made a point of it when revealing his new product at a New York City press conference held on November 19, 2007. As reported by Erick Schonfeld liveblogging for Techcrunch .com, "Jeff Bezos takes the stage: Shows a [cuneiform] tablet, then some papyrus, then a codex, a picture of Gutenberg ('invented mass production of books,' thanks Jeff)."[2] After briefly recapping this history, he unveiled

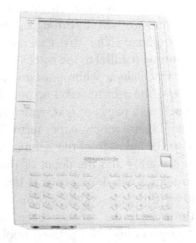

Figure 4.1. First generation Amazon Kindle, 2007. RIT Cary Graphic Arts Collection. Photograph by Elizabeth Lamark.

what he banked on would be the future of reading technology—Amazon's version of the e-reader. Not only did the Kindle join the long evolution of the history of the book, but it also borrowed and repurposed a few of the most important historical book technologies.

Whether deliberatively designed to be this way or not, the first-generation Kindle derives functions from at least four vital communication technologies in the history of the book. First and foremost, the Kindle is, as it was first advertised, a handheld tablet. This plastic device reaches far back 5,000 years to its clay ancestors from ancient Mesopotamia. It is larger than the average cuneiform tablet, which on average was closer to the size of a credit card, but certainly clay tablets survive that approach the 7.5×5.3 inch, 10.4 ounces of the Kindle. A Sumerian tablet from c. 2100 BCE held in the Cary Collection, for example, is not much smaller (see figure 1-3). The Kindle is a portable device made of plastic with a rubber backing, designed to be read while held in one's hand. Its size makes its use easy in almost any setting.

The Kindle also harkens back to another ancient technology—the roll or scroll. The use of papyrus as a surface for writing appeared in around 3000 BCE in ancient Egypt, where papyrus grew along the banks of the Nile River. As they evolved, rolls were also made from a more geographically accessible material, parchment (the skin of animals such cows, goats, and sheep). The linear nature of rolls or scrolls gives us the modern, digital verb to "scroll" through a page, whether on a computer screen or a smartphone. The first-generation Kindle includes a scrolling feature. Running parallel to the right side of the screen is a scroll bar, at the bottom of which sits a white plastic cylinder that serves as a scroll wheel. This allows the user to scroll up and down menus. This function is not used as much with pages of text, which tend not to run off the page or "below the fold," to use a newspaper term. The wheel and the scroll bar did not survive the redesign of the Kindle 2.

By 2007 and the debut of the Kindle, the codex structure was over a millennia old, dating back to the wax tablets of ancient Greece and Rome. Over time, the codex became the book format familiar to most readers throughout the world. Since the introduction of page numbers over 500 years ago, the printed book has taught readers to think about and quantify text in terms of pages. So ingrained is the book's structure, not only do most modern readers count what they have read by page numbers, but they also have an innate desire to physically turn pages. The first-generation Kindle accommodated our reliance on pages by presenting digital texts as collections of pages that needed to be turned. This virtual turning of the page is activated physically by pressing the very long button on the device's right side that reads "NEXT PAGE," or the two smaller buttons on the left side that read "PREV PAGE" and "NEXT PAGE." Placing these buttons on both sides of the tablet reflects the physical choices of turning forward or backward in a book, with a clear emphasis on moving forward by turning the page on the right side, as if it were the recto page. In this way, the first-generation Kindle imitated the functions of the printed book to accommodate readers who were used to turning pages and absorbing texts in terms of numbers of pages.

One last technology was incorporated into the first-generation Kindle. This technology is so very common in our daily use of mobile devices and personal computers that it might be easy to overlook. The Kindle was designed to be an interactive device, so it needed a method for inputting text. The method chosen was the QWERTY keyboard, a natural choice as it had been used in English-speaking countries for well over a century, first with typewriters and then with personal computers. In fact, the QWERTY keyboard was patented by Christopher Latham Sholes in 1878. Although it might seem odd that readers are still using a 19th-century system from a now antiquated writing technology, the QWERTY keyboard remains a very popular method of inputting data, particularly in the United States. Analog QWERTY keyboards were present on the first three generations of Kindle; the Kindle 4 evolved beyond having it as a part of its design.

The first-generation Kindle's historical self-awareness is illustrated physically on the backside of the tablet. As shown in figure 4-2, embossed into the device's soft gray rubber backing are characters that illustrate the history of letterforms. Starting in the upper left corner appear hieroglyphic and cuneiform characters—some of the first systems of writing. Descending and expanding outward are more letterforms: Hebrew and Greek characters, and the early Roman letters that survive in ancient stone

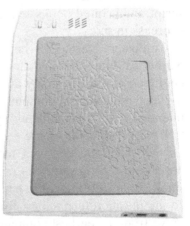

Figure 4-2. Back of Amazon Kindle, 2007. RIT Cary Graphic Arts Collection. Photograph by Elizabeth Lamark.

inscription. We then find examples of the blackletter script that character-ize manuscript books in medieval Europe, followed but the roman letter-forms that were revived and refined in print during the European Renaissance. At the end of this cascade of characters, we arrive at truly modern san serif typefaces. This evolution of letterforms from the Middle East and Europe mirrors the evolution of the book.

The first-generation Kindle—a brief history of the book in one device. Of course, there is an exciting history of tablets that predates the Kindle, so let us take a step backward and look at the recent evolution that led the way to modern tablet computers and e-readers.

THE HISTORY OF THE BOOK = A HISTORY OF SIZE

Size is a strong theme in the history of the book. Size is often the first indicator of how a book would have been used by its readers. A large folio Bible (a public book meant to be read on a table or lectern) versus an octavo New Testament or Book of Psalms (a private book held in the reader's hand and read wherever there was sufficient light). Throughout the history of writing and reading technology, there is usually a trend toward smaller, handheld devices. Some devices like clay tablets and scrolls started out small and did not have much smaller to go. Manu-script and printed books tended to start off in the larger size and then decrease in size.

Computers started off huge. Take, for example, ENIAC (Electronic Numerical Integrator and Computer). Constructed from 1943 to 1945 by engineers at the University of Pennsylvania, ENIAC was a groundbreak-ing electronic digital computer—one of the first of its kind.[3] No pun is intended with "groundbreaking," but it certainly works that way, too. ENIAC filled 1,500 square feet and weighed in at 30 tons.[4] *A Brief His-tory of the Book* does not tackle the history of computers, except to observe that, for a variety of reasons, there was an evolution from large to small, from institutional to personal, and, in the context of the history of communication technology, this happened very fast. The time it took to move from the earliest computers such as ENIAC to the rise of personal computers of the 1970s is merely three decades. From personal comput-ers to tablet computers and smartphones is less than half a century. Con-sidering the longer history explored thus far, this history is a blip, but it is a profound blip.

PERSONAL COMPUTERS

The rise of personal computers, or PCs, began in earnest in the late 1970s. The Apple I, developed by Steve Jobs (1955–2011) and Steve Wozniak (1950–), debuted in 1976. In 1977 both the Commodore PET and TRS-80 were released, as well as the Apple II. PCs could be used comfortably at work and at home. This is not to say that computers did not stay large. Super computers have continued to develop alongside of personal computers, processing data at amazing speeds for purposes that are well beyond the needs of the average person.

Pausing for a moment on the word "computer," our discussion returns ever so briefly to ancient clay tablets. At a glance, the two media might not seem related, but their original purposes were similar. The first clay tablets were typically used to take inventories—for counting. As discussed in Chapter One, it is for this reason that the earliest cuneiform texts were mostly nouns and numbers.[5] Computers were first used for exactly what the name meant—computing. They were machines that performed calculations. Early clay tablets and early computers were initially both calculators. Just as clay tablets evolved, so too did computers, and dramatically so. Computers evolved so much and so very quickly that most users do not think of computers as "computers." The definition of "computer" from the *Oxford English Dictionary* is helpful:

> An electronic device (or system of devices) which is used to store, manipulate, and communicate information, perform complex calculations, or control or regulate other devices or machines, and is capable of receiving information (data) and of processing it in accordance with variable procedural instructions (programs or software); esp. a small, self-contained one for individual use in the home or workplace, used esp. for handling text, images, music, and video, accessing and using the Internet, communicating with other people (e.g., by means of email), and playing games.[6]

"Handling text" and "playing games" came pretty early in the history of personal computers. Most of the computer functions related to the Internet found in that last sentence of the *Oxford English Dictionary* definition came later in the brief history of personal computers—handling "images, music, and video, accessing Internet, communicating with other people."

Not too long after the growing availability of the personal computer came portable computers (also called suitcase computers at the time). In a

1981 article in *The New York Times,* Portia Isaacson of Future Computing is quoted as saying "I think the portable computers will take off like gang-busters." She further predicted that "businessmen will soon be carrying entire electronic offices with them, consisting of microcassette recorders, tiny printers, tiny televisions and small keyboards all attachable to a small computer."[7] In hindsight, Isaacson's description paints a somewhat humorous picture of a miniature office with tiny components and microcassettes, but her vision was not too far off the mark. The technology that she lists evolved rather quickly or, in the case of microcassettes, grew obsolete. Yet when we think of current technology, our tablet computers and smartphones cover pretty much all the functions of "electronic offices." This technology, however, needed a few decades to evolve to its current state.

PORTABLE COMPUTERS EN ROUTE TO TABLETS

A step in this evolution toward modern tablets and smartphones was first handheld or pocket computers. One such device introduced to the market in 1980 was the Tandy/Radio Shack or TRS-80 PC. The "PC" in this case stands for "pocket computer." Known also as the PC1, the TRS-80 PC was the pocket version of the popular TRS-80 personal computer.[8] An advertisement for the PC2 drives home the futuristic nature of a pocket computer with the endorsement of professor and science fiction writer Isaac Asimov (1920–1992), who boldly announces, "A few years ago, the idea of a computer you could put in your pocket was just science fiction."[9]

So what did these "pocket-sized" computers do? What were they used for? A Radio Shack salesman in a 1982 *Financial Times* article explains,

> We sell the pocket calculator to students who use it to learn program-
> ming, to airline pilots for in-flight calculations, to real estate brokers
> for making loan and payment calculations on the spot, and to scien-
> tists from Stanford University who use it for field calculations. . . .
> The pocket computer is easier to programme than a programmable
> calculator because you can use an established computer language
> like basic [sic].[10]

This use of "pocket calculator" rather than "pocket computer" in this statement is intriguing. Perhaps it was a misprint? Was it a Freudian slip? "Pocket calculator" speaks to the fact that the first pocket computers were to most users, "glorified calculators," to quote a reviewer in an 1984 article in *InfoWorld*.[11] In the same article on "hand-held micros" such as the

TRS-80 PC, another reviewer noted, "For the non-engineer, there aren't any applications."[12] Applications were and still are crucial factors for the sale and use of computers. These portable, pocket-sized computers had memory, which was a good step, but users were looking for new applications that took advantage of the machine's size. And they had not yet arrived. By 1984, sales of the portable computer had declined. One commentator predicted that "The market won't take off until the lap-size computer takes off."[13] In hindsight, this statement is pretty prescient. Laptops, like IBM Thinkpads introduced in 1990, would be very successful in a way that pocket-sized computers never really were. Note the phrase used, "lap-size computer." "Laptop" was not yet in common parlance in 1984. The earliest uses cited in the *Oxford English Dictionary* date back to 1983.[14]

Yet development of pocket-sized computers continued. One of the technologies that helped pocket computers evolve was pen computing—that is, an interface that allowed the user to control their computer with a pen. A 1990 article on pen computing from the *Sun Herald* in Sydney, Australia, begins: "Even if you have never used a keyboard, there may be a personal computer in your future."[15] A year later in the *Globe and Mail*, a consultant notes "Some people are more comfortable with writing . . . a lot of people who see a keyboard get phobic."[16] A 1985 commercial for Pencept's PenPad 200 talks about interacting with their product in a "natural style" and with fewer steps than a keyboard and mouse.

Younger readers might forget that typing was not a natural act for many early computer users—it was a skill that just a few decades ago was not as widespread as it is today. Many digital natives have grown up with the QWERTY keyboard constantly at their fingertips as one of their primary means of communication. Generation X and older might have taken a typing class at one point in their lives, and it might have been on a typewriter. Using a pen to input information into a computer (and it is perhaps more accurately called a stylus) takes us back to the very earliest tablets made of clay and wax. Today's stylus is, of course, most often our own index fingers.

PERSONAL DIGITAL ASSISTANTS

Pen computing did not take hold. Rather, a mouse and a keyboard became the most common conduits for inputting information. The stylus, however, did find use in the operation of the first personal digital assistants (PDAs). Apple, for example, released one of the first commercial PDA tablets in

Figure 4-3 Apple Newton MessagePad 100, 1994. RIT Cary Graphic Arts Collection. Photograph by Elizabeth Lamark.

1993—the MessagePad or the Apple Newton. Figure 4-3 shows a third generation Newton from 1994. Expectations were quite high for this tablet. In May 1992, Apple CEO John Sculley announced, "This is the beginning of the biggest thing Apple has ever done. Our goal is to be the Johnny Appleseed of this new market for highly personalised devices that you can carry around in your pocket."[17] In hindsight, this announcement might seem both pretentious and prescient. The Newton was ultimately not a very successful product. Yet, the idea of a PDA being the "biggest thing Apple has ever done" rings true, even if that "new market of highly personalised devices" would ripen about 15 years or so in the future. At the time, however, the Newton was marketed as "The astonishing new invention that has room for your whole world but fits in your pocket."[18] It managed your calendar, sent faxes, and allowed the user to write and draw—all of these functions in a pocket-sized product. This claim, too, might have been overreaching. Newtons are about the size of a video cassette and, despite the proclivity for baggy clothes in the early 1990s, it was unlikely that pockets could comfortably fit the device. Nevertheless, the Newton held the promise of portability and usability—the latest handheld, portable reading device in the millennia-old evolution of communication media.

One of the factors that was going to drive the success of the Newton was its handwriting recognition feature. Users could input information into the Newton using a stylus, and the tablet would interpret their handwriting. Unfortunately, this feature might not have worked as well as they had hoped. In America, people and products were sometimes judged by how they were portrayed in episodes of the cartoon *The Simpsons*. The Newton famously appeared in the *Simpsons*' episode, "Lisa on Ice," from 1994, and it did not fare very well. The kids are at a school assembly. The bully Kearney says to Dolph, "Take a memo on your Newton. Beat up Martin." This is what Dolph writes on his Newton, but the Newton interprets the text as "Eat Up Martha." In frustration Dolph chucks his Newton and hits Martin in the head.[19]

In addition to problems with handwriting recognition, the Newton's overall utility was a problem. As the *Financial Times* put it in 1994, "This seems to be a technology that is searching for a useful application."[20] This point seems key. What could this PDA really do, and who was it really aimed at? The users' guide touted time zone responsiveness and currency calculations. You could beam information such as your business card to nearby Newtons or PCs that were set up to receive information. You could fax information using a modem. Such functions seem to indicate businesspeople, not your average users. The price also was a barrier. The first Newton retailed between $700–$1,000.[21]

Despite the Newton's drawbacks, the essentials of the modern version of the handheld tablet were present. In terms of readability/writability, users could input text with a stylus, and if they wanted to erase what they had written, they could just scribble out the text and it would disappear in a dramatic puff of smoke. The information written could be saved, transferred onto a computer, or shared with another user. In many ways, the Apple Newton had laid important groundwork for future PDAs and tablet computers.

THE PALM PILOT

Introduced by Palm Inc. in 1996 with the Palm 1000, the Palm Pilot was a successful handheld that actually fit quite easily in a user's hand. Its design and functions were focused on basic core utilities. The Palm Pilot, shown in figure 4-4, offered an address book, calendar, notepad, and calculator—all functions related to personal and professional organization. The Palm was priced at a more reasonable $299.

Like the Newton, the Palm Pilot was operated with a stylus. Handwriting recognition on the Palm Pilot took a different and ultimately more practical approach. Rather than attempting to distinguish personal styles, the Palm functioned with a handwriting recognition that demanded every user learn and utilize a regularized set of characters. This system, called Graffiti, reduced letters and numbers to uniform, readable characters. As figure 4-5 shows, some of the letters were to be written exactly as would be expected. Other letters, such as the A, F, and T, were distilled to an essence of the original letters. In this way, users of the Palm Pilot were expected to learn new characters for some of the alphabet. Yet, doing so was surprisingly easy, as completing the activity below will show. If users

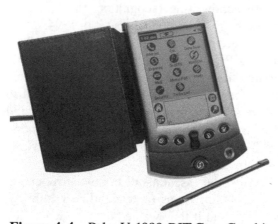

Figure 4-4   Palm V, 1999. RIT Cary Graphic Arts Collection. Photograph by Elizabeth Lamark.

Figure 4-5   Graffiti is the handwriting recognition system for Palm PDAs. RIT Cary Graphic Arts Collection. Photograph by Elizabeth Lamark.

did have trouble adapting, they had a tried-and-true backup. They could always call up a QWERTY keyboard on their screen and input text in that manner.

Successfully inputting text with a stylus on the Palm using Graffiti required users to modify how they wrote. Users were adapting to the device—abstracting their writing to make it more efficient for the writing medium. This modern human/tablet adaption reflects the ancient human/tablet adaption as evidenced in the example of the evolution of the symbol for barley in cuneiform shown in Chapter One of *A Brief History of the Book*. Millennia before writers learned Graffiti on the Palm Pilot, ancient writers adapted complicated strokes to simple abstract strokes that worked more efficiently on the clay tablet. In the history of the book there are moments like this when humans adapt their behavior to the needs of technology, rather than technology being adapted to human needs.

DIFFERENT DEVICES FOR DIFFERENT USES

In the early 2000s, the popularity of handheld devices was not pervasive, and their ownership depended on the needs of their users. Some users needed an e-mail pager (which BlackBerry introduced in 1999), some needed a PDA, and some needed a cell phone (which had grown in popularity in the late 1990s). Of course, there were some users who needed all three devices. Readers of *A Brief History of the Book* might be old enough to remember seeing people wearing various devices holstered on their belts like some geeky version of Batman. This controversial tablet fashion style was nicknamed "bat-belt syndrome." It was born of the lack of one device that could perform all the operations that users required from handhelds.

Tying together the needs of modern handheld users were devices like the Palm Treo, introduced in 2002 and, shortly thereafter, a BlackBerry model featuring a cell phone. As *Computerworld* noted in 2002, the Palm Treo removed "the necessity of carrying a BlackBerry, a cell phone and a Palm organizer by providing a single device that offers the best features of all three."[22]

This was, and remains, a dangerous combination. Early on in the history of modern handhelds, users were noting the addictive nature of these devices. The BlackBerry quickly earned the nickname CrackBerry, as those who owned them seemed never to be able to put them down. A passage from a 2003 article written by George Emerson for the *Globe and Mail* reported on this phenomenon and, in the process, described a tablet-related, human behavior that has grown all too familiar:

> With BlackBerry in hand, like a Geiger counter sniffing for radiation, I began to detect hidden moments of downtime I once used for daydreaming. I began to read and write e-mails while riding in elevators and standing in airport lineups. I discovered an entire life of downtime in front of my television. Soon it was a challenge to stop e-mailing while driving.[23]

The modern handheld was born, and with it a new addiction to downtime screen use. It appears that the inclusion of a cell phone was a crucial driver of the popularity of handheld devices. It was the one function that was and continued to be pervasive. As devices incorporated a phone, one of the most basic of our technological needs, their popularity grew. For example, according to the Pew Research Center, 65 percent of Americans owned a cell phone in 2004. In 2013 that percentage was 91 percent, while the number of *smartphone* owners in 2013 was 61 percent. As of 2018, 77 percent of Americans owned a smartphone.[24] Times keep changing, of course. By 2012, making phone calls was the fifth most-used function on smartphones. According to a UK survey, the order was as follows: "1. Browsing the internet 2. Checking social networking sites 3. Playing games 4. Listening to music 5. Making calls 6. Emails 7. Text messaging 8. Watching TV/films 9. Reading books 10. Taking photographs."[25] Phone calls came in at the halfway point, while reading books finished second to last on this list. For users of smartphones, other functions had grown in popularity: interacting with audio and video content, taking photos with digital cameras, and, of course, access to all the World Wide Web had to offer. But for those who wanted technology for the explicit use of reading books, there were many options. Evolving alongside PDAs and tablet computers were e-books and e-readers.

BOOKS OPERATED THROUGH COMPUTERS

An e-book may be generally defined as a book "distributed in an electronic format."[26] There are various ways e-books can be distributed and read, whether through a computer, e-reader, tablet computer, or a smartphone. From their earliest days onward, e-books not only expanded the ways that books could circulate, but they often innovated the traditional functions of a book.

Innovation extended even to literary genre. Take, for example, hypertext fiction. In 1990, Eastgate Systems published one of the first works of hypertext fiction, Michael Joyce's *afternoon, a story*.[27] As with other titles published by Eastgate, *afternoon, a story* was packaged in a way that made it appear like a normal-sized, albeit thin, paperback book. The Cary Collection has several Eastgate titles that, when shelved side-by-side, look very much like a series of printed paperbacks. As customary for printed books, the spine of *afternoon, a story* displays from top to bottom, the author, title, and publisher. The front cover is also designed like a printed book, displaying the author, title, a photo (in this case of the author), and a blurb from *The New York Times Book Review*. Open the "book," however, and you are greeted not with pages, but with a pocket folder of sorts that houses a user's manual and a diskette (3 1/2-inch floppy disk). *afternoon, a story* was designed to be read on a personal computer using a "hypertext authoring system" called Storyspace. Works of hypertext fiction are generally not linear in the traditional literary sense but, through taking advantage of digital technology, are written to be interactive. Readers decide where to go in the novel, following links to different modules of text and media. Pioneering hypertext novels such as *afternoon, a story* and Shelley Jackson's *Patchwork Girl* continue to be read and studied.

Books also found their way onto CD-ROMs. As with hypertext fiction, the opportunities afforded by presenting texts in a digital medium rather than print allowed publishers to present "extended books" on CD-ROMs. As Walt Crawford explained in *American Libraries*, "Extended e-books, either on CD-ROM or the Web, go beyond printed books in a number of ways besides offering searchable text. Good CD-ROMs can help users explore some topics in ways not supported by ordinary books, and the same is true for innovative Web-based resources."[28] The Voyager Company, for example, produced a series of extended books on CD-ROM. The first in their Voyager Shakespeare series was an edition of *Macbeth*, released in 1994. As with the packaging of hypertext fiction, Voyager CD-ROMs also came in boxes that resembled printed books. Yet they sought to offer much more than just the texts, serving up a multimedia experience that supplemented the written word. In the case of Voyager's *Macbeth*, augmenting Shakespeare's Scottish play are traditional textual annotations and reference works such as a concordance, as well as more innovative supplementary material such as film clips, audio performances from the Royal Shakespeare Company, and a media gallery, and *Macbeth* Karaoke, which "allows you to choose a role, and act scenes from the play with professional actors."

The presentation of books, whether just the text or "extended" with additional content also migrated onto the web, where readers could access them freely online. The texts chosen were usually those in the public domain, so that copyright would not be an issue. *Project Gutenberg*, for example, was founded in 1971 by Michael S. Hart (1947–2011) with the mission of making public domain written works accessible as electronic versions. With the advent of the World Wide Web, this mission grew dramatically, as more volunteers helped upload more and more titles.[29] As of December 2019, *Project Gutenberg* hosts 60,923 free books to be read onscreen, printed out, or downloaded to an e-reader. Books found on *Project Gutenberg* are text-based, though some are enhanced with book covers and illustrations from early editions.

Of course, the World Wide Web offered manifold opportunities to enhance books in sophisticated ways. By the late 1990s, the groundbreaking presentation of *Macbeth* by the Voyager Company was mirrored by websites like *The Interactive Shakespeare Project at Holy Cross*.[30] Produced in

1998–1999 as a by-product of a National Endowment for the Humanities teaching institute held at the Folger Shakespeare Library in Washington, DC, *The Interactive Shakespeare Project* presents a comprehensive, multimedia edition of Shakespeare's *Measure for Measure*. The full text of the play is enhanced with essays, annotations, and discussion questions, as well as movie clips for each scene. All of this content was made freely available for readers to interact with online or print out on paper.

The World Wide Web was not the only site for reading e-books. Readers were not limited to their desktop and laptop computers to access e-books. As the web developed its presence as a book provider, the written word was also concurrently moving to electronic handheld devices that catered to more traditional reading behavior.

ELECTRIFYING THE BOOK[31]

From the ancient world to the present, readers have gravitated to handheld, portable books. It should come as no surprise that e-readers—devices

specifically dedicated to reading books—would emerge in the later part of the 1990s alongside PDAs. E-book readers or e-readers are handheld portable devices that serve up electronic books. They are what Clifford Lynch in 1999 called "a book-reading appliance."[32] As we have seen, consumers of books did not necessarily need a specific electronic device for reading books, which could be bought or borrowed in print, or served up and read in a variety of ways on desktop or laptop computers (and later on tablets or even on smartphones). E-readers, however, offered a means of storing and reading e-books in ways that had a more natural affinity with traditional reading habits. Not only were e-readers designed primarily for interacting with books and other reading material such

Figure 4-6 NuvoMedia's Rocket eBook, 1998. RIT Cary Graphic Arts Collection.

as magazines or newspapers, but they were physically designed to be small and lightweight (though with a large enough screen to comfortably display text). They were portable like paperbacks, but could store many more titles at once.

Two of the earliest e-readers were introduced in 1998: the Rocket eBook (figure 4-6) by NuvoMedia and the Softbook Reader by Softbook Press Inc. A reviewer from *Computer World* named David Strom tried out these two devices shortly after their release, along with the Millenium E-Reader and EB Dedicated Reader. Strom "found them all lacking."[33] "None was as comfortable to read as a printed page," he argued, noting that "All had limited content available."[34] Other users, however, were finding that e-readers offered features not available in printed books. Reporting on the use of Rocket eBooks at Algonquin Public Library in 2000, Roberta Burke observed that:

> As the number and variety of our electronic titles have grown, so, too, has the number of interested patrons. Such features as backlighting, adjustable-size type, a built-in dictionary, and the ability to "pack" many books into a portable 22-ounce reader make them appealing beyond simple curiosity. . . . Since November, the library has included a short survey with each Rocket Reader when it is checked out. Patron response has been overwhelmingly positive. They like the backlighting, they like the portability, they like trying something new.[35]

E-readers added new functionality to the traditional book, while also transforming the codex form into a modern handheld with a structure that harkened back to, and expanded on, historical book technology.

A NEW BOOK STRUCTURE

E-readers converted the structure of a codex with leaves bound along the long edge into a rectangular plastic tablet that held a screen for displaying text. The size of early e-readers was consistent with traditional handheld reading devices. The Rocket eBook measured about the size of a paperback book with a 3×4.5 inch screen. It weighed 22 ounces. It cost $499. An optional leather case (bookbinding for a digital device, I suppose) cost an additional $119. The Softbook was a larger device that featured a 6×8 inch screen and weighed 2.9 pounds.[36] The Softbook cost

$299, but with a monthly subscription of $20. Both devices had a rounded left edge to help it fit comfortably in the reader's hand.

The Rocket eBook and Softbook both used LCD screens, but e-reader displays were about to undergo a technological innovation that made the experience of using an e-reader more akin to reading a printed book. In 1996, MIT undergraduate Barrett Comiskey (1975–) and MIT professor Joseph Jacobson (1965–) filed a patent for a nonemissive display (as opposed to a self-lit, emissive display such as an LCD screen).[37] Though not listed on the patent, MIT undergraduate J. D. Albert (1975–) was also involved in the invention. A year later, the three inventors founded the E Ink Corporation. Their electrophoretic, nonemissive display produced a screen that appears very much like ink on traditional paper, is thin like traditional paper, and requires very little power to use. As Paul Smalera of the *Saturday Evening Post* declared in 2009, "It's these traits that make E Ink displays nearly perfect as a reading medium."[38] The technology works as follows:

> In black-and-white e-paper, each pixel is made up of around 60 plastic microcapsules that contain a negatively charged black powder and a positively charged white powder. To make a pixel black, electrodes underneath the display apply a negative charge to push the black powder to the top. To reproduce shades of grey, some electrodes are positive and others negative, so some microcapsules are white while others in the same pixel are black. Once a page is set, this arrangement uses no power—critical for reading book-length content.[39]

Released in 2004, the Sony Librie was the e-reader that introduced E Ink's e-paper to the reading public. As one reporter noted at the time, "The text on Sony's new Librie electronic book reader doesn't quite equal ink on a page in clarity, but it comes remarkably close. It's easier on the eyes than any electronic display yet."[40] Still, the same reviewer asked, "Whether such lightweight digital ink-based tablets eventually supplant newspapers, magazines, paperbacks and hardcovers, we'll have to see."

In the early 2000s, e-readers were still a burgeoning technology. One contemporary discussion of e-books contrasted them with printed books by using a term for paper books that clearly did not catch on—"p-books."[41] At this point, there was still the larger question of whether "portable e-books" were "a viable reading option."[42] A more comfortable design and access to more and more content were not too far ahead. Strom's 1999 e-reader review quoted above was titled "E-Books: Still an Unfinished

Work." The "finishing" of e-readers would continue through the development of devices such as the Sony Reader (2006), eventually culminating in 2007 with the success of the first generation of Amazon's Kindle and then onto other popular e-readers such as Barnes & Noble's Nook (2009), the PocketBook (2009), and the Kobo eReader (2010).

While e-paper became the foundation for most e-readers, LCD screens remained the choice for tablets and smartphones such as the iPad and iPhone. It was perhaps inevitable that the functions of e-readers and tablets would eventually intersect. As Jason Griffey noted in 2012 in *Library Technology Reports*, "Both Amazon and Barnes and Noble have moved past the E Ink readers to make e-reader models that have traditional LCD screens. These products, the Barnes and Noble Nook Color and Nook Tablet and the Amazon Kindle Fire blur the line between e-reader and tablet, with some functionality from each."[43] In 2019, functionality and technology continue to blur—as e-readers can be a hybrid of technologies. The Amazon Oasis, for example, features e-paper and an LCD for fine-tuning the screen, while the Barnes & Noble Nook Glowlight adds an LED light for reading in the dark. This is all an indication that readers continue to interact with texts in a variety of places and through a variety of formats.

WORLD WIDE WEB

Readers across the globe also increasingly interact with the written word through the World Wide Web. A 2019 study from the United Nations' International Telecommunication Union (ITU) found that "Internet use has expanded to 54 per cent of the global population" or roughly 4.1 billion people.[44] More locally, a survey from the Pew Research Center shows that in 2018, 90 percent of Americans were online and interacting with the Internet.[45]

The development of the World Wide Web has undoubtedly been the most profound recent development in the history of communication. The design of websites and their presentation of text and image is an evolution that is about 30 years old, and yet, due to the speed of this evolution, a great deal has changed in just a short amount of time. Looking at the evolution of websites after reading the first three and a half chapters of *A Brief History of the Book*, readers will recognize that history repeated itself once again. In fact, the early history of website design mirrored the broader history of the evolution of the book from tablets, to rolls or scrolls, to codices.

Readers of *A Brief History of the Book* who were early active Internet users can attest to how ugly, clunky, and hard to use the first websites truly were. You might think of glittery banners, animated construction worker GIFs alerting visitors that the site was "under construction," unicorns JPGs, and grating MIDI versions of the Eagles' classic "Hotel California." You might remember Webrings found at the bottoms of web pages that helped connect users to similar websites. This period of design can be viewed as the incunabula period of the World Wide Web. Just as in the first 50 years following the invention of printing in the West, printed books first imitated manuscripts and then evolved into their own forms, through the first 10 years or so of the development of the World Wide Web, websites imitated previous media for a period before breaking away more dramatically from the past. The incunabula period of websites might be defined as the World Wide Web going live on August 6, 1991, to the beginnings of "Web 2.0" as coined and defined by Darcy DiNucci in 1999 (see discussion below).

The anniversary of the public World Wide Web is popularly celebrated on March 12 because on the day that in 1989 Sir Tim Berners-Lee of CERN "wrote a paper proposing a system of servers, hyperlinks and other technologies that make the web possible."[46] Berners-Lee is therefore considered the inventor of the World Wide Web. A second important anniversary date related to the World Wide Web is August 6, 1991—the appearance of the first web page. The earliest screenshot of this web page was taken in 1992. CERN has preserved it here: http://info.cern.ch/hypertext/WWW /TheProject.html. It reads, "The WorldWideWeb (W3) is a wide-area hypermedia information retrieval initiative aiming to give universal access to a large universe of documents."

This first web page might bring to mind an ancient clay tablet—a small, rectangular contained surface imparting a minimal amount of text. Or maybe it might evoke a simple leaf or page from a book (certainly it would be called a web *page*). Either way, it was the beginning of a new era in the history of written and graphic communication.

What really separated this new reading and writing technology from those that came before it was hyperlinking, that is, the ability to link to other web pages containing information. This is the world of hypertext. The OED definition is helpful, defining hypertext as, "Text which does not form a single sequence and which may be read in various orders." CERN's first web page linked to another CERN page that defined hypertext, a term which in 1991 would have been quite new to most everyone:

What is hypertext?

- Hypertext is text which is not constrained to be linear.
- Hypertext is text which contains links to other texts. The term was coined by Ted Nelson around 1965 . . .
- HyperMedia is a term used for hypertext which is not constrained to be text: it can include graphics, video, and sound, for example. Apparently, Ted Nelson was the first to use this term too.
- Hypertext and HyperMedia are concepts, not products.[47]

In the history of the book there are two main modes of access: rolls or scrolls enabled *linear* access, clay and wax tablets and codices enabled *random* access. Hypertext and hypermedia dramatically amplify random access. With a codex you can jump from page to page, or to book to book, depending on your resources. Through the World Wide Web, you can jump to thousands or even millions of different texts. Hypertext is hyper access, and it is increasingly jousting with the random access provided by traditional printed book formats, just as random access once jousted with the linear access of rolls.

Reading was a function of the World Wide Web from the very start. A book from 1994 titled *Everybody's Guide to the Internet* begins with a list of some of the Internet's functions:

- stay in touch with friends, relatives, and colleagues around the world, at a fraction of the cost of phone calls or even air mail;
- discuss everything from archaeology to zoology with people in several different languages;
- tap into thousands of information databases and libraries worldwide;
- retrieve any of thousands of documents, journals, books, and computer programs;
- stay up-to-date with wire-service news and sports and with official weather reports;
- play live, "real-time" games with dozens of other people at once.[48]

Although decades old, this early list of Internet uses is pretty telling (though perhaps some of its omissions might be surprising today). Access to "documents, journals, books," and "news" demonstrates that reading was an important use of the World Wide Web even in its earliest days.

INCUNABULA WEBSITES

Exploring the early days of the World Wide Web and examining the incunabula of the Internet is an adventure aided by websites such as the *Internet Archive*. This extraordinary resource is

a digital library of Internet sites and other cultural artifacts in digital form. Like a paper library, we provide free access to researchers, historians, scholars, the print disabled, and the general public. Our mission is to provide Universal Access to All Knowledge. We began in 1996 by archiving the Internet itself, a medium that was just beginning to grow in use.[49]

Thanks to the *Internet Archive*'s early mission, access to many first-generation websites has been preserved. Browsing its Wayback Machine can be quite an exciting tour of the early years of web design. Another website, *Internet Archaeology*, has a similar mission, seeking "to explore, recover, archive and showcase the graphic artifacts found within earlier Internet Culture. Established in 2009, the chief purpose of *Internet Archaeology* is to preserve these artifacts and acknowledge their importance in understanding the beginnings and birth of an Internet Culture." It is through resources like this that we can study the incunabula period of web design.[50]

As we have seen, the very first web page from CERN resembled a tablet or perhaps a parchment or paper leaf. The web pages that followed were undoubtedly scrolls—digital descendants of ancient papyrus rolls. Early web designers could link to information but, perhaps because linking was a new behavior in the history of reading, they often chose to put the majority of the web page's content below the fold, or in digital terms, beneath the bottom of the screen. Readers would have to scroll beyond the visible page to view the content below.

For a fun exercise, use *Internet Archaeology*'s "Web Grabs" to experience early sites such as *All the Dogs in My Life*.[51] While perhaps an extreme example, this is undoubtedly an Internet scroll! There is a tremendous amount of information to scroll through—as there were many dogs in the life of this website author. This was not uncommon in early web design. But designers soon learned that users did not want to scroll. Plus the time it took for multiple images to load on screen back in the early days of the World Wide Web meant that the more graphics you put onto one scrolling page, the longer it took for the page to fully load. I cannot imagine how long all the graphics in "All the Dogs in My Life" would have taken to appear on screen back in the 1990s.

Scrolling web pages presented linear information intermixed with hyperlinks. The next step, naturally, was to try to imitate the codex. This was affected by using a design style called frames. Take, for example, *The World's Worst Website*, a site "designed to graphically demonstrate the most common mistakes made by new Web Page designers" (http://www.angelfire.com/super/badwebs). If the flashing images or the moving text is not charming enough, be sure to press play on the audio player to hear a 16-second MIDI version of "The William Tell Overture" repeat interminably. Although clearly a satirical take on frames design, this website does provide a good example of how frames worked. At the top there is a static title, similar to running titles that you see at the top of the pages in a printed book. On the left side is a narrow frame that serves as a table of contents in the form of links. When you chose a link, that content then appears in the larger right frame that serves as the main reading area. Thus the content of the top frame and left frame do not change, only the content in the larger right frame. In this way, the right frame served the function of a page of a book, while the links in the left frame served the function of turning those pages. Sometimes, in addition to the links in the left frame, a website using frames might include "Forward" and "Back" buttons for browsing—a clear nod to moving forward and backward in a book by physically turning pages. While frames is not an often recommended style of design, variations of frames can work well when presenting literary texts. Take, for example, Dartmouth's *John Milton Reading Room* and its presentation of Milton's *Paradise Lost*.[52] Here, a frames design is successful for organizing and presenting Milton's great epic.

Thus far, web pages have echoed tablets, scrolls, and books. What would they do now? Following frames, web designers increasingly created web pages on which all the content fit onscreen, with links to additional content. Sometimes these links were found on hot areas of images using an image map. With this simpler sort of design, websites began to move out of their incunabula period.

Web design next moved into a new period christened Web 2.0—a term coined by Darcy DiNucci who, in 1999, wrote:

The Web we know now, which loads into a browser window in essentially static screenfuls, is only an embryo of the Web to come. The first glimmerings of Web 2.0 are beginning to appear, and we are just starting to see how that embryo might develop. . . . The Web will be understood not as screenfuls of text and graphics but as a transport mechanism, the ether through which interactivity happens.[53]

DiNucci's predictions came to fruition. Over the subsequent 20 years, the World Wide Web has become less static, more social, interactive, and multimedia. While the first websites presented text and image in modes not too far off from their print and manuscript ancestors, websites evolved into a new form that expanded on the capabilities of past media. When DiNucci wrote that "Today's Web is essentially a prototype—a proof of concept," this idea reflected the idea that the Web was still drawing on the features of various book forms from the past, and was now ready to evolve.

RETURN TO THE SCROLL?

Yet, despite all of this innovation, modern readers using digital devices have returned to the scroll. This is mostly due to responsive web design, that is, designing web content that performs well across platforms— whether on a desktop or laptop computer, or smaller devices such as smartphones and tablet computers. Because users access information using a number of different devices, designers need to design websites for multiple platforms. If a website is designed to fit on the larger screens of desktop computers or laptops, the content might end up quite small on smartphones. This often requires readers to magnify the text by using the two-fingered, pinch-to-zoom gesture on most touchscreens. To avoid information getting lost on smaller screens, responsive web design uses a flexible layout that can fill screens of every size. So, for example, a wide grid layout on a laptop screen might condense to a single column on a smartphone.

Responsive web design is not a new phenomenon. In December 2012, a *Mashable* article titled "Why 2013 Is the Year of Responsive Web Design" explained why the website made dramatic changes to their design. Author Pete Cashmore wrote, "Today, 30% of Mashable's traffic is mobile. By the end of next year, this may exceed 50%." Even as early as 2013, popular websites saw that the majority of their users were, or would soon be, primarily mobile users. They needed to accommodate these users. Today, it is estimated that 51 percent of global Internet users are accessing the web only with their smartphones. It is predicted that by 2025 that percentage will rise to nearly 75 percent.[54]

Responsive design on a smartphone tends to have graphic features and text presented in a column that scrolls down to further content—not dramatically scrolling like *The Dogs of My Life* website, per se, but scrolling in a more controlled, organized manner. Scrolling vertically or even swiping horizontally is a gesture that works quite well on smartphones and tablets, and has become second nature to many users.

If handhelds like tablets and smartphones have become our chief communication technology, and scrolling a common gesture when reading, has the history of the book come full circle back to reading behaviors of the ancient world?

THE FUTURE: PRINT AND DIGITAL

The behaviors learned from operating smartphones and tablets have not remained limited to the digital world. When examining the history of the book, as we have done through *A Brief History of the Book,* it becomes clear that different book forms influenced each other and not always in a chronological fashion. The printed book imitated the manuscript book and then developed its own features. In return, manuscript books borrowed new features from the printed book. For example, if you see a 16th-century European manuscript that has a title page or page numbers, you are seeing the influence of printed books on a manuscript book.

It might not be surprising then that the printed book might borrow qualities from tablets, computers, and smartphones. Take, for example, the Dutch dwarsligger or flipback book format.[55] The word "dwarsligger" means "to lie crossways."[56] True to this definition, this construction of these books reworks the traditional codex, so that the lines of text run parallel to the book's spine rather than perpendicular. In this format, the pages are flipped up vertically rather than turned over horizontally. The paper used in a dwarsligger book is very thin, making it possible for the reader to hold the book and flip pages up using just one hand. In this way, the format of this new style of the printed book imitates reading behavior performed on a smartphone or tablet.

In 2018, for example, Dutton Books for Young Readers published a boxed set of four John Green novels for the Penguin Minis series. The blurb from the back of the box reads, "The Penguin Minis revolutionary landscape design and ultra-thin paper makes it easy to hold in one hand without sacrificing readability. Perfectly-sized to slip into a pocket or bag, Penguin Minis are ideal for reading on the go."[57] A review from *The New York Times* makes the connection between the dwarsligger or flipback and current digital reading devices:

> The tiny editions are the size of a cellphone and no thicker than your
> thumb, with paper as thin as onion skin. They can be read with one

hand—the text flows horizontally, and you can flip the pages upward, like swiping a smartphone. . . . It's a bold experiment that, if successful, could reshape the publishing landscape and perhaps even change the way people read.[58]

Will the influence of digital devices successfully inspire new book formats "that reshape the publishing landscape and perhaps even change the way people read?" Dwarsligger or flipback books incorporate features from several book technologies. Their operation returns us to wax tablets as handled by the Greeks. Their format is a bound printed book but adapted to the behavior of smartphone users. Physical reading and writing formats will undoubtedly continue to evolve and find inspiration in the latest digital technologies. The history of books from cuneiform to Kindle has demonstrated over and over again that readers desire handheld, portable books. But might we also eventually break away from the physical nature of reading?

AUGMENTED AND VIRTUAL REALITY

Future directions for reading might be less concerned about physical objects—whether a printed book or an e-reader—and more interested in the space that surrounds us. Augmented reality (AR) and virtual reality (VR) are both relatively young technologies that could have a major impact on how readers interact with text and images. AR is a mixture of the real and virtual worlds facilitated through the use of a digital device. AR took a leap forward in1996 with the release of Pokémon Go—a popular (and free) AR game that had people using their devices to find Pokémon characters hiding throughout the world around them. Librarians at RIT even discovered an Abra hiding in the Cary Collection!

AR is already being used in book publishing. There are examples of printed children's books that include AR content that is activated by looking at the pages through a phone or tablet. *iDinosaur* published in 2018 by Carlton Books, for example, allows the reader to engage an AR feature that brings each dinosaur to life. Not only are the dinosaurs illustrated on the printed page, but a 3D animated version moves around the page.[59] A coloring book being developed by Disney features enhanced digital content that turns the characters on the page into 3D animated characters as the child colors them.[60]

These examples show AR as a way of augmenting the traditional reading experience via a printed book, but might AR technology offer new ways of reading that no longer require a printed book or digital reading device? Whether using AR or VR, interacting with the space around us currently requires a device to mediate. Such as device does not have to be a handheld. Wearable digital technology, for instance, began to make an impact in 2013 with the introduction of Google Glass smart glasses. In addition to offering functions such as taking photos, browsing the web, and finding directions on a map, Rob Salkowitz of *Publishers Weekly* saw reading in AR as a future application for Google Glass:

> It's not hard to imagine an app for Glass that recognizes printed texts that the user is reading; this would allow the Glass wearer to overlay, hyperlink, and annotate the texts in digital space, effectively blending the physical and digital. Or perhaps Glass could just superimpose digital texts over blank pages in physical books, combining the hard-to-replace tactile experience of reading a nice printed edition with the conveniences (and distractions) of an e-book.[61]

Google Glass has not yet become as popular as some predicted it would, and no such reading application for smart wear has yet to come to fruition. A new line of smart glasses, Amazon Echo Frames, released in 2019, does not appear to have even an AR feature, nor any functions related to reading. They are more of a PDA interacting with Alexa.[62]

VR is an immersive technology. Using a virtual reality headset and system such as Vive or Oculus Rift, users enter a virtual world, travel to different places, and interact with objects, including books. How might this immersive technology intersect with reading and bring about new reading experience? Libraries and museums are increasingly experimenting with VR to facilitate access to historical artifacts and works of art. For example, as of 2019, the Cary Collection is developing the Virtual Cary Collection, the aim of which is for users to experience being in a 3D model of the library's reading room and handling 3D models of rare and unique artifacts. Digitizing a cultural object opens up new possibilities for deeper study that might be challenging or impossible with the real object. For example, one of the artifacts chosen for the Virtual Cary Collection is the English hornbook, c. 1600, shown in figure 3-22. Users in the Virtual Cary Collection handle the hornbook, examine it, and read its text, just as they would with the thing itself. In the virtual world, however, users are able to interact with the hornbook in ways that they cannot in the real world. For example, users may take the hornbook apart and study its parts, view a simulation in which the hornbook de-ages back to how it would have likely looked when it was first created, and travel back to a location and time in which the hornbook would have been used—in this case a 16th-century schoolhouse. To augment the learning experience, books about hornbooks could be digitized and made available to the user, if he or she feels compelled to read more about the history of these devices.

In this way, VR opens up enhanced reading experiences that allow the users to explore the historical context of a book. This is appropriate for the setting and mission of a rare book library, but might VR enhance or change our everyday reading experiences? There are a number of VR apps available that offer environments specifically aimed at readers. Chimera Reader, for example, offers various VR reading environments that help block out everyday distractions and enhance the reading experience. Settings include reading in a study, a cozy bedroom, or a library. Of course, VR could also be used to immerse the reader in an environment that enhances the plot or mood of a story. A writer for the website *Book Riot* describes using a Vive and the application Bigscreen to access his desktop computer and an e-book version of a Stephen King short story while in VR. He then set the VR environment so he could read the story by a campfire, and found the experience "amazing."[63] I suspect my daughter would relish the opportunity to read her *Harry Potter* books in various Hogwarts settings (and, yes, so would I). E-readers have also gone virtual. An immersion VR reader, for example, is an e-reader that users can operate in VR to read books stored in a virtual library. The users can also choose from various environments in which to read.[64]

VR is also being used to enhance the content of books and perhaps attract new readers. Author Romina Russell complemented her *Zodiac* series with a VR experience that expands on the text of her books, and allows interaction with other readers and the author herself as an avatar.[65] If the user has not yet read the books, perhaps the VR experience will inspire them to begin, or read more of, the series.

All in all, AR and VR are both still very much in their early stages of development and not yet finding mainstream popularity. A poll from 2017 found that "16% and 9% of Americans have tried VR and AR, respectively."[66] Those numbers are increasing, of course, especially as the cost of VR systems such as Vive and Oculus Rift have become more affordable.

How these technologies will continue to develop and add to the greater evolution of reading is yet to be seen.

ACTIVITY

Activity 5: Mastering Graffiti on a Palm

Objective

Readers will gain experience using the Palm Pilot, one of the first successful personal digital assistants (PDAs). By learning to input text using Palm's handwriting recognition system, Graffiti, readers will discover the importance of handwriting recognition and how users of the Palm had to adjust their writing to be successful on this device.

Supplies

- Several working Palm models. Palms can be acquired rather inexpensively, and you might even have success soliciting donations.
- Printouts of the Graffiti's alphanumeric gestures. These are easily found online, or copy the one illustrated in figure 4-5.

Instructions

1. Power up the Palm.
2. Spent a few minutes getting familiar with the tablet.
3. Navigate to the "Learn Graffiti" module and take the tutorial.
4. After taking the tutorial, explore the various functions of the Palm.
5. Spend time writing using Grafitti in the "Memo Pad" or "To Do List" applications.

ASSIGNMENTS

Assignment 1

Write a page reflecting on the experience of using a Palm. What useful features and applications does the Palm have or lack? How does the Palm compare to modern smartphones, tablets, or devices?

Assignment 2

Complete activity "Making and Using a Cuneiform Tablet" from Chapter One. Write a page reflecting on your experiences using both the cuneiform tablet and Palm devices. How are these handheld tablets similar and/or dissimilar?

NOTES

1. http://news.bbc.co.uk/2/hi/technology/7107118.stm.

2. https://techcrunch.com/2007/11/19/liveblogging-the-amazon-kindle-e-reader-show-with-jeff-bezos.

3. For a scholarly history of ENIAC, see Thomas Haigh, Mark Priestley, and Crispin Rope, *ENIAC in Action: Making and Remaking the Modern Computer* (Cambridge, MA: MIT Press, 2016).

4. "ENIAC," in *Dictionary of Energy* (2nd ed.), ed. C. Cleveland and C. Morris (Oxford, UK: Elsevier Science & Technology). https://ezproxy.rit.edu/login?url=https://search.credoreference.com/content/entry/este/eniac/0?institutionId=3255.

5. Eleanor Robson, "The Clay Tablet Book in Sumer, Assyria, and Babylonia," in *A Companion to the History of the Book*, ed. Simon Eliot and Jonathan Rose (Malden, MA: Blackwell, 2007), 68.

6. "computer, n.," OED Online, December 2019, Oxford University Press. https://www-oed-com.ezproxy.rit.edu/view/Entry/37975?redirectedFrom=computer (accessed December 16, 2019).

7. Andrew Pollack, "Technology: The Portable Computer," *New York Times,* March 26, 1981, Thursday, Late City Final Edition.

8. See also the Sharp PC-1211.

9. This ad can be seen here: https://medium.com/the-molten-mind-space/science-fiction-science-as-craft-44c5776f6704.

10. Louise Kehoe, "Portable Computer Sales Expected to Soar," *Financial Times* (London), September 7, 1982, Tuesday.

11. Kathy Chin, "Hand-Held Micros Lose Hold," *InfoWorld*, February 13, 1984, 59.

12. Ibid.

13. Ibid., 61.

14. "laptop, n. and adj.," OED Online, July 2018, Oxford University Press. http://www.oed.com.ezproxy.rit.edu/view/Entry/57210613 (accessed October 14, 2018).

15. David Frith, "NEXT, PCS WITH PENS FOR NOTE SCRIB-BLERS," *Sun Herald* (Sydney, Australia), July 29, 1990, Sunday.

16. Mary Gooderham, "Electronic Notebook Gives New Meaning to 'User Friendly,'" *The Globe and Mail*, July 19, 1991; ProQuest Historical Newspapers, A1.

17. Louise Kehoe, "Feel the Force—Apple Will Today Unveil Newton, an Electronic Gadget Which It Claims Will Help You Take Control of Your Life," *Financial Times* (London), May 29, 1992, Friday.

18. See advertisement illustrated here: https://www.theregister.co.uk/Print/2013/09/17/20_years_of_the_apple_newton.

19. https://www.cnet.com/news/the-simpsons-eat-up-martha-was-the-first-autocorrect-fail.

20. Louise Kehoe, "Digital Assistant Is of Limited Help—Apple's MessagePad Is a Revolutionary Computer but Could Struggle to Find a Useful Role," *Financial Times* (London), August 5, 1993, Thursday.

21. Ibid.

22. Michael Gartenberg, "Treo Merges the Best of Three Worlds," *Computerworld* 36.5 (2002): 21.

23. George Emerson, "You Sexy Thing; the New BlackBerry 6710 Is an E-mail/Cellphone Combination That's Nothing Less Than a Fetish Object," *Globe and Mail* (Canada), January 31, 2003, Friday.

24. https://www.pewinternet.org/fact-sheet/mobile.

25. https://www.dailymail.co.uk/sciencetech/article-2166603/Making-calls-fifth-used-function-smartphones—web-Facebook-games-music.html.

26. "e-book, n.," OED Online, December 2019, Oxford University Press.   https://www.oed.com/view/Entry/254154?redirectedFrom=e-book (accessed December 22, 2019).

27. Some consider it to be the first; see Phil Brooks, "The Death of the Hypertext Novel and What We Can Learn from Its Failure to Launch," 2010, Order No. 1477017, Northern Illinois University. https://ezproxy.rit.edu/login?url=https://search.proquest.com/docview/520383391?accountid=108.

28. Walt Crawford, "Nine Models, One Name: Untangling the E-Book Muddle," *American Libraries* 31.8 (2000): 59.

29. For a history of *Project Gutenberg*, see Marie Lebert Project Gutenberg (1971–2008). https://www.gutenberg.org/ebooks/27045.

30. http://college.holycross.edu/projects/isp/index.html.

31. This heading is taken from the title of the article: Clifford A. Lynch, "Electrifying the Book, Part I," *NetConnect*, Supplement to *Library Journal* 124: 17 (October 1999): 3–6.

32. Ibid., 3.

33. David Strom, "E-Books: Still an Unfinished Work," *Computerworld* (July 19, 1999), 76.

34. Ibid.

35. Roberta Burke, "Don't Be Afraid of E-Books." *Library Journal* 25.7 (2000): 42.

36. Crawford, 56.

37. https://worldwide.espacenet.com/patent/search/family/024967261 /publication/US5930026A?q=pn%3DUS5930026.

38. Paul Smalera, 2009, "E-Books: A Good Read," *Saturday Evening Post* 281.5: 19.

39. Paul Marks and Michael Fitzpatrick, "Hues Are Going to Love the Next Generation of E-Readers," *New Scientist* 202.2708 (2009): 22.

40. Yuri Kageyama, "REVIEW: Sony E-Book a Revolution for Eyes," *Associated Press Online*, June 30, 2004, Wednesday.

41. Kim Zetter, "Pulp Friction: E-Books Take on Paper," *PC World* 18.11 (2000): 56.

42. Ibid., 42.

43. Jason Griffey, "E-Readers Now, E-Readers Forever!" *Library Technology Reports* 48.3 (2012): 16.

44. "UN: Global Internet Use Quadrupled since 2005, but Gender Gap Growing," Deutsche Presse-Agentur, November 5, 2019, Tuesday. See also https://www.itu.int/en/ITU-D/Statistics/Documents/facts/FactsFigures 2019.pdf.

45. https://www.pewresearch.org/internet/fact-sheet/internet-broadband.

46. https://www.pbs.org/newshour/nation/recalling-early-days-world -wide-web; http://info.cern.ch/Proposal.html.

47. https://www.w3.org/History/19921103-hypertext/hypertext/WWW /WhatIs.html.

48. Adam Gaffin, *Everybody's Guide to the Internet* (Cambridge, MA: MIT Press, 1994), ix.

49. https://archive.org/about.

50. http://internetarchaeology.org/index.htm.

51. http://internetarchaeology.org/webgrabs.htm. Choose number 28.

52. http://www.dartmouth.edu/~milton/reading_room/pl/book_1 /text.shtml. Hat tip to https://webstyleguide.com/wsg2/page/frames.html.

53. Darcy DiNucci, "Fragmented Future," *Print* 53.4 (1999): 32.

54. https://www.cnbc.com/2019/01/24/smartphones-72percent-of-people -will-use-only-mobile-for-internet-by-2025.html.

55. For a brief, animated video on this format, see https://vimeo.com /207102685.

56. https://www.mnn.com/lifestyle/arts-culture/stories/dwarsligger-flip back-book.

57. John Green, *John Green: Mini Collection* (New York: Dutton Books, 2018).

58. https://www.nytimes.com/2018/10/29/business/mini-books-pocket -john-green.html.

59. Carlton Books, *iDinosaur* (AR), 2018. https://www.carltonbooks.co .uk/idinosaur-ar-hb.html.

60. https://youtu.be/SWzurBQ81CM.

61. Rob Salkowitz, "The Future of Reading: 10 Trends for 2014 and Beyond," *Publishers Weekly* 261.3 (2014): 25.

62. For a preview see Michael Brown, "Amazon Echo Frames: Hands-on First Impressions," *PCWorld* 37.11 (2019): 70–72.

63. https://bookriot.com/2018/03/10/reading-in-virtual-reality-the-good -and-not-so-good.

64. https://immersionvr-reader.com.

65. https://www.techrepublic.com/article/how-vr-creates-an-immersive -experience-for-readers.

66. http://www.econtentmag.com/Articles/Editorial/Feature/Virtual -Augmented-and-Mixed-Reality-Opens-Up-a-World-of-Possibilities-for -Publishers-117723.htm.

Bibliography

Aldhelm, Saint. *The Riddles of Aldhelm. Text and Verse Translation with Notes by James Hall Pitman.* Hamden, CT: Archon Books, 1970.

Avrin, Leila. *Scribes, Script and Books: The Book Arts from Antiquity to the Renaissance.* Chicago: American Library Association; London: British Library, 1991.

Backhouse, J. "Lindisfarne Gospels." *Grove Art Online.* 2003. https://www.oxfordartonline.com/groveart/view/10.1093/gao/9781884446054.001.0001/oao-9781884446054-e-7000051172 (accessed November 9, 2019).

Bagnall, Roger S., ed. *The Oxford Handbook of Papyrology.* Oxford; New York: Oxford University Press, 2009.

Balston, J. N. *The Whatmans and Wove Paper: Its Invention and Development in the West.* West Farleigh, Kent: John Balston, 1998.

Banham, Rob. "The Industrialization of the Book, 1800–1970." In *Companion to the History of the Book,* edited by Simon Eliot and Jonathan Rose, 273–290. Malden, MA: Blackwell, 2007.

Barbier, Frédéric. *Gutenberg's Europe: The Book and the Invention of Western Modernity.* Chicester, West Sussex, England: Polity Press, 2016.

Bennett, H. S. *English Books & Readers 1603–1640; Being a Study in the History of the Book Trade in the Reigns of James I and Charles I.* Cambridge, England: Cambridge University Press, 1969.

Brown, Michael. "Amazon Echo Frames: Hands-on First Impressions." *PCWorld* 37.11 (2019): 70–72.

Bülow-Jacobsen, Adam. "Writing Materials in the Ancient World." In *The Oxford Handbook of Papyrology,* edited by Roger S. Bagnall, 3–29. Oxford; New York: Oxford University Press, 2009.

Burke, Roberta. "Don't Be Afraid of E-Books." *Library Journal* 25.7 (2000): 42–45.

Campbell-Kelly, Martin, William Aspray, Nathan Ensmenger, and Jeffery R. Yost. *Computer: A History of the Information Machine*. Boulder, CO: Westview Press, 2014.

Casson, Lionel. *Libraries in the Ancient World*. New Haven, CT: Yale University Press, 2001.

Charpin, Dominique. *Reading and Writing in Babylon*. Cambridge, MA: Harvard University Press, 2010.

Chin, Kathy. "Hand-Held Micros Lose Hold." *InfoWorld*, February 13, 1984, 59–62.

Clemens, Raymond, and Timothy Graham. *Introduction to Manuscript Studies*. Ithaca, NY: Cornell University Press, 2007.

Companion to the History of the Book. Edited by Simon Eliot and Jonathan Rose. Malden, MA: Blackwell, 2007.

Cook, Scott D. N. "Technological Revolutions and the Gutenberg Myth." In *Internet Dreams: Archetypes, Myths, and Metaphors*. Edited by Mark Stefik. Cambridge, MA: MIT Press, 1997.

Crawford, Walt. "Nine Models, One Name: Untangling the E-Book Muddle." *American Libraries* 31.8 (2000): 56–59.

David, Paul A. "Clio and the Economics of QWERTY." *The American Economic Review* 75.2 (1985): 332–337.

Davies, Martin. *Aldus Manutius: Printer and Publisher of Renaissance Venice*. Tempe, AZ: Arizona Center for Medieval and Renaissance Studies, 1999.

De Hamel, Christopher. *Scribes and Illuminators*. Toronto: University of Toronto Press, 1992.

De Hamel, Christopher. *The Book. A History of the Bible*. London; New York: Phaidon, 2001.

Derolez, Albert. *The Palaeography of Gothic Manuscript Books: From the Twelfth to the Early Sixteenth Century*. Cambridge, UK; New York: Cambridge University Press, 2003.

DiNucci, Darcy. "Fragmented Future." *Print* 53.4 (1999): 32, 221–222.

Edgren, J. S. "China." In *A Companion to the History of the Book*, edited by Simon Eliot and Jonathan Rose, 97–110. Malden, MA: Blackwell, 2007.

Elsky, Martin. *Authorizing Words: Speech, Writing, and Print in the English Renaissance*. Ithaca, NY: Cornell University Press, 1989.

Emerson, George. "You Sexy Thing; the New BlackBerry 6710 Is an E-Mail/Cellphone Combination That's Nothing Less Than a Fetish Object." *Globe and Mail* (Canada). January 31, 2003, Friday.

Fiddyment, Sarah, Bruce Holsinger, Chiara Ruzzier, Alexander Devine, Annelise Binois, Umberto Albarella, Roman Fischer, et al. "Animal Origin of 13th-Century Uterine Vellum Revealed Using Noninvasive Peptide Fingerprinting." *Proceedings of the National Academy of Sciences of the United States of America* 112.49 (2015): 15066–15071. https://www.ncbi.nlm.nih.gov/pmc/articles /PMC4679014.

Finkel, Irving, and Jonathan Taylor. *Cuneiform*. Los Angeles: J. Paul Getty Museum, 2015.

Franklin, Benjamin. *The Autobiography of Benjamin Franklin*. Edited by Leonard W. Labaree. New Haven, CT: Yale University Press, 1964.

Frith, David. "Next, Pcs with Pens for Note Scribblers." *Sun Herald* (Sydney, Australia). July 29, 1990, Sunday.

Gaffin, Adam. *Everybody's Guide to the Internet*. Cambridge, MA: MIT Press, 1994.

Galbraith, Steven K. *Edges of Books*. Rochester, NY: Cary Graphic Arts Press, 2012.

Galbraith, Steven K. "English Literary Folios 1593–1623." In *Tudor Books and Readers: Materiality and the Construction of Meaning,* edited by John N. King, 46–67. Cambridge: Cambridge University Press, 2010.

Galbraith, Steven K. "Latimer Revised and Reprised: Editing *Frutefull Sermons* for Pulpit Delivery." *Reformation* 11 (2006): 29–46.

Gartenberg, Michael. "Treo Merges the Best of Three Worlds." *Computerworld* 36.5 (2002): 21.

Gaskell, Philip. *A New Introduction to Bibliography*. New York; Oxford: Oxford University Press, 1972.

Gaudet, John J. *Papyrus: The Plant That Changed the World, from Ancient Egypt to Today's Water Wars*. New York: Pegasus Books, 2014.

Gaul, Albro Tilton. *The Wonderful World of Insects*. New York: Rinehart, 1953.

Green, John. *John Green: Mini Collection*. New York: Dutton Books, 2018.

Greenfield, Jane. *ABC of Bookbinding: A Unique Glossary with over 700 Illustrations for Collectors & Librarians*. New Castle, DE: Oak Knoll Press; New York: Lyons Press, 1998.

Griffey, Jason. "E-Readers Now, E-Readers Forever!" *Library Technology Reports* 48.3 (2012): 14–20.

Gullick, Michael. "How Fast Scribes Write." In *Making the Medieval Book: Techniques of Production*, edited by Linda L. Brownrigg. Los Altos Hills, CA: Anderson-Lovelace, 1995.

Haigh, Thomas, Mark Priestley, and Crispin Rope. *ENIAC in Action: Making and Remaking the Modern Computer.* Cambridge, MA: MIT Press, 2016.

Hunter, Dard. *Papermaking: The History and Technique of an Ancient Craft.* New York: Dover Publications, 1978.

Hye-Bong, Ch'on. "Pulcho Chikchi Simch'e Yojol." *Korean Journal* 3 (1963): 12.

Jenkins, Caitlin. "Making Papyrus in the Conservation Lab." Brooklyn Museum.org. July 2010. https://www.brooklynmuseum.org/comm unity/blogosphere/2010/07/08/making-papyrus-in-the-conservation -lab (accessed August 11, 2018).

Johnson, Elmer D. *History of Libraries in the Western World.* Metuchen, NJ: Scarecrow Press, 1970.

Kageyama, Yuri. "REVIEW: Sony E-Book a Revolution for Eyes." *Associated Press Online.* June 30, 2004, Wednesday.

Kehoe, Louise. "Digital Assistant Is of Limited Help—Apple's Message-Pad Is a Revolutionary Computer but Could Struggle to Find a Useful Role." *Financial Times* (London). August 5, 1993, Thursday.

Kehoe, Louise. "Feel the Force—Apple Will Today Unveil Newton, an Electronic Gadget Which It Claims Will Help You Take Control of Your Life." *Financial Times* (London). May 29, 1992, Friday.

Kehoe, Louise. "Portable Computer Sales Expected to Soar." *Financial Times* (London). September 7, 1982, Tuesday.

Koops, Matthias. *Historical Account of the Substances Which Have Been Used to Describe Events, and to Convey Ideas, from the Earliest Date to the Invention of Paper.* London: Printed by Jacques and Co., 1801.

Kornicki, Peter F. *The Book in Japan: A Cultural History from the Beginnings to the Nineteenth Century.* Leiden, Netherlands; Boston: Brill, 1998.

Kornicki, Peter F. "Japan, Korea, and Vietnam." In *A Companion to the History of the Book*, edited by Simon Eliot and Jonathan Rose, 111–125. Malden, MA: Blackwell, 2007.

The Lanston Monotype: Two Articles on the Lanston Monotype Machine Reprinted from the Pages of the Inland Printer. Rochester, NY: Press of the Good Mountain, 1970.

Lapidge, Michael. 2004. "Aldhelm [St Aldhelm] (d. 709/10), Abbot of Malmesbury, Bishop of Sherborne, and Scholar." *Oxford Dictionary of National Biography.* December 24, 2018. http://www.oxforddnb.com/view/10.1093/ref:odnb/9780198614128.001.0001/odnb-9780198614128-e-308.

Lundmark, Torbjörn. *Quirky Qwerty: The Story of the Keyboard @ Your Fingertips.* UNSW, Sydney, NSW: UNSW Press, 2002.

Lynch, Clifford A. "Electrifying the Book, Part I," *NetConnect.* Supplement to *Library Journal* 124: 17 (October 1999), 3–6.

Lyons, Martyn. *Books: A Living History.* Los Angeles: J. Paul Getty Museum, 2011.

Marcou, David J. "Korea the Cradle of Movable Metal Type." *Korean Culture* 13.1 (1992): 4–6.

Marks, P. J. M. *The British Library Guide to Bookbinding: History and Techniques.* London: British Library, 1998.

Marks, Paul, and Michael Fitzpatrick. "Hues Are Going to Love the Next Generation of E-Readers." *New Scientist* 202.2708 (2009): 22.

McKenzie, D. F. *Bibliography and the Sociology of Texts.* London: British Library, 1986.

Moran, James. *Printing Presses: History and Development from the Fifteenth Century to Modern Times.* Berkeley: University of California Press, 1973.

Mowery, J. Franklin. "Clasps, Schliessen, Clausuren. A Guide to the Manufacture and the Literature of Clasps." *Guild of Book Workers Journal* 24.2 (1991): 1–58.

Murdock, Kathryn. "Make Your Own Wax Tablet and Stylus." *Calliope* 9.3 (November 1998).

Murphy, Denis J. *People, Plants, and Genes: The Story of Crops and Humanity.* Oxford; New York: Oxford University Press, 2007.

Netz, Reviel, and William Noel. *The Archimedes Codex: How a Medieval Prayer Book Is Revealing the True Genius of Antiquity's Greatest Scientist.* Philadelphia: Da Capo Press, 2007.

Netz, Reviel, et al. *The Archimedes Palimpsest.* Cambridge; New York: Published for the Walters Art Museum by Cambridge University Press, 2011.

Oxford Handbook of Cuneiform Culture. Edited by Karen Radner and Eleanor Robson. Oxford; New York: Oxford University Press, 2011.

Pafort, Eloise. "Notes on the Wynkyn De Worde Editions of the 'Boke of St. Albans' and Its Separates." *Studies in Bibliography* 5 (1952): 43–52.

Parkinson, R. B. *Papyrus.* London: British Museum Press, 1995.

Payton, Robert. "The Ulu Burun Writing-Board Set." *Anatolian Studies* 41 (1991): 99–106.

Petroski, Henry. *The Book on the Bookshelf.* New York: Alfred A. Knopf: Distributed by Random House, 1999.

Pollack, Andrew. "Technology; the Portable Computer." *New York Times.* March 26, 1981, Thursday, Late City Final Edition.

Pollard, Graham. *Changes in the Style of Bookbinding, 1550–1830.* London; New York: Oxford University Press, 1956.

Priest-Dorman, Greg, and Carolyn Priest-Dorman. "Making and Using Waxed Tablets." https://www.cs.vassar.edu/~capriest/tablets.html.

Riederer, Rachel. "Archaeologists Discover Trove of Cuneiform Tablets in Northern Iraq." Smithsonian.com. October 24, 2017. https://www.smithsonianmag.com/smart-news/archaeologists-cuneiform-tablets-northern-iraq-180966923.

Roberts, Colin H., and T. C. Skeat. *The Birth of the Codex.* London; New York: Published for the British Academy by the Oxford University Press, 1983.

Robson, Eleanor. "The Clay Tablet Book in Sumer, Assyria, and Babylonia." In *A Companion to the History of the Book*, edited by Simon Eliot and Jonathan Rose, 67–83. Malden, MA: Blackwell, 2007.

Roemer, Cornelia. "The Papyrus Roll in Egypt, Greece, and Rome." In *A Companion to the History of the Book*, edited by Simon Eliot and Jonathan Rose, 84–94. Malden, MA: Blackwell, 2007.

Romano, Frank J. *History of the Linotype Company.* Rochester, NY: RIT Press, 2014.

Rouse, Richard H., and Mary A. Rouse. "Wax Tablets." *Language & Communication* 9.2.3 (1989): 175–191.

Salkowitz, Rob. "The Future of Reading: 10 Trends for 2014 and Beyond." *Publishers Weekly* 261.3 (2014): 24–25.

Schuyler, Montgomery. "Notes on the Making of Palm-Leaf Manuscripts in Siam." *Journal of the American Oriental Society* 29 (1908): 281–283.

Scora, Peter E., and Rainer W. Scora. "Some Observations on the Nature of Papyrus Bonding." *Journal of Ethnobiology* 11.2 (1991): 193–202.

Sigrist, Marcel. *Documents from Tablet Collections in Rochester New York*. Bethesda, MD: CDL Press, 1991.

Smalera, Paul. 2009. "E-Books: A Good Read." *Saturday Evening Post* 281.5: 19–70.

Smith, Margaret M. *The Title-Page, Its Early Development*, 1460–1510. New Castle, DE: Oak Knoll Press, 2000.

Smith, Margit J. *The Medieval Girdle Book*. New Castle, DE: Oak Knoll Press, 2017.

Sohn, Pow-key. "Early Korean Printing." *Journal of the American Oriental Society* 79.2 (1959): 96–103.

Stallybrass, Peter. "Books and Scrolls: Navigating the Bible." In *Books and Readers in Early Modern England: Material Studies*, edited by Jennifer Andersen and Elizabeth Sauer, 42–79. Philadelphia: University of Pennsylvania Press, 2002.

Stallybrass, Peter, Roger Chartier, J. Franklin Mowery, and Heather Wolfe. "Hamlet's Tablets and the Technologies of Writing in Renaissance England." *Shakespeare Quarterly* 55.4 (2004): 379–419.

Strom, David. "E-Books: Still an Unfinished Work." *Computerworld*, July 19, 1999, 76.

Szirmai, J. A. *Archaeology of Medieval Bookbinding*. Aldershot, Hants; Brookfield, VT: Ashgate Publishing, 1999.

Taylor, Jonathan. "Tablets as Artefacts, Scribes as Artisans." In *Oxford Handbook of Cuneiform Cultures*, edited by Karen Radner and Eleanor Robson, 5–31. Oxford; New York: Oxford University Press, 2011.

Thompson, Stephen E. "Egyptian Book of the Dead: Document Analysis ca. 1569–1315 BCE." In *Milestone Documents of World Religions*. Salem Press, 2017. https://ezproxy.rit.edu/login?url=https://search.credoreference.com/content/entry/greymdwr/egyptian_book_of_the_dead_document_analysis_ca_1569_1315_bce/0?institutionId=3255.

Twyman, Michael. *The British Library Guide to Printing: History and Techniques*. Toronto: University of Toronto Press, 1998.

United States Patent Office. *Annual Report of the Commissioner of Patents: Report of the Commissioner of Patents, for the Year 1845*. Washington, DC: Ritchie & Heiss, print, 1846.

White, Eric Marshall. *Editio princeps: A History of the Gutenberg Bible*. London; Turnhout: Harvey Miller Publishers, 2017.

Wilson, Penelope. *Hieroglyphs: A Very Short Introduction*. Oxford; New York: Oxford University Press, 2004.

Xenophon. *Cyrupaedia: The Institution and Life of Cyrus, the First of that Name, King of Persians*. London: Printed by J. L. [i.e. John Legate] for Robert Allot . . . 1632.

Zamorensis, Rodericus. *Epistola de expugnatione Nigropontis*. Cologne: Ulrich Zel, about 1470–1471.

Zetter, Kim. "Pulp Friction: E-Books Take on Paper." *PC World* 18.11 (2000): 56.

Index

About the Author

STEVEN K. GALBRAITH, PHD, is curator of the Cary Graphic Arts Collection at Rochester Institute of Technology (RIT) and former Andrew W. Mellon Curator of Books at the Folger Shakespeare Library in Washington, DC. He is coauthor of Libraries Unlimited's *Rare Book Librarianship*. Dr. Galbraith teaches Tablet to Tablet: A History of the Book at RIT.

Printed in the USA
CPSIA information can be obtained
at www.ICGtesting.com
LVHW021618201223
766876LV00003B/112

9 781440 869396